Grow RICH With Diamonds

Investing in the world's
most precious gems

Grow RICH With Diamonds

Investing in the world's most precious gems

by
Bernhard Dohrmann

Published in San Francisco by
Harbor Publishing
Distributed by G. P. Putnam's Sons

For information contact Harbor Publishing, 1668 Lombard Street,
San Francisco, California 94123.

Printed in the United States of America.

Compositor—Turner, Brown & Yeoman
Printer & Binder—Fairfield Graphics
Cover Designer—Catherine Hopkins
Copyeditor—Judy Johnstone

ISBN No. 0-936602-29-5

SPECIAL NOTE TO READERS

This publication is intended to present the author's experiences
and is sold with the understanding that the author is not engaged
in rendering legal, accounting or other professional service. The
services of a competent professional should be sought for legal or
other expert assistance.

The author specifically disclaims any personal liability for any
loss or risk incurred as a consequence of any use, direct or indirect,
of advice or information contained in this publication.

DEDICATION

"Grow Rich With Diamonds" has been dedicated to the ultimate prosperity and welfare of Jennifer Ann Dohrmann (age 6) and Jason Alan Dohrmann (age 2). Without their love this book could not have been written . . . and it is their love that, like the diamond itself, is forever!

CONTENTS

Preface

Y ou may already be diamond rich!

Four out of five brides in America today receive a diamond engagement or wedding ring. Most families own one or more diamonds set in contemporary jewelry or in heirlooms. If you or someone in your family has a diamond, chances are excellent that it's worth hundreds, and probably thousands, of dollars more than was originally paid for it.

The reason for this is diamond appreciation. There is nothing in the world to compare to it! *For years diamonds have been steadily increasing in value at a rate that exceeds the rate of inflation.* A study recently conducted by a leading financial firm not connected with the field charted diamond growth between 1905 and 1975 (see Chapter 6 for details). It concluded that diamonds appreciated at an average annual rate of 12 percent a year during that time despite two World Wars, the Great Depression and numerous recessions. The appreciation rate since 1975 has been far, far greater.

Your diamond, the one on your ring or in your pendant or in your safety deposit box, is growing in value as you read this. Yet it is the safest investment you could own, possibly even safer than an insured bank account. Unlike paper money, diamonds cannot be printed indiscriminately by a government and thereby have their value diluted. Unlike gold, diamonds cannot be debased by adding copper or other nonprecious metals. Unlike gold and silver, diamonds are not subject to the great upswings and downswings of a speculative market. Unlike stocks, bonds and T-bills, diamonds are inflation positive after taxes. Unlike real estate, diamonds are liquid—you can always get your money out. Unlike any of these, diamonds have a track record of *thousands* of years of value with steady, stable appreciation.

Even more than this, diamonds can grant you the power to survive. What if a global war were actually to break out? What if oil supplies were suddenly cut off from the Middle East? What if a virulent new crop disease cut our food supplies to a quarter of their present yield? What if America should experience another financial panic and find its economy set back a hundred years? All of us act as if it could never happen, but it could. And what if it did?

Diamonds could allow you to survive and even prosper. During the tragic days in Germany after the First World War, people were starving and there was little shelter because of the bombing, but those who had diamonds were able to buy a side of beef, a suit of clothes or a warm, dry place to sleep. Paper money bought nothing. Gold, because it had been debased, frequently was not accepted. Diamonds were.

Diamonds have bought milk for a baby when none was to be found. Diamonds have been used to bribe border guards. Diamonds have bought a horse or a car when one was needed to escape. Diamonds are the oldest survival "money" in the world. Hundreds of years before Christ the forces of Alexander the Great ravaged India in a vain search for diamonds, so well-known was their value.

Because they provide a means to survive, diamonds are in reality a kind of financial time machine. They have the power to carry their owners across a time of great peril. With the world in economic chaos, diamonds would have the power to transport our wealth—and our very selves—into the next century.

This book explains in detail the two great properties of diamonds: their steady and enduring appreciation, historically far in excess of inflation, and their function as a time machine to insure our survival. But there is far more.

This book will also tell you why the diamond in your jewelry is going to be worth far more tomorrow than it is today.

2

It will explain why the value of diamonds moves *steadily* upward.

It will show you how the DeBeers syndicate acts to keep the price of diamonds *down* (not up, as so many people think).

It will explain how petrodollar investors, pension fund managers, and wealthy individuals have "discovered" diamonds and are now quietly buying them up.

It will show how you can buy diamonds for substantial profits with little or no risk.

It will explain diamond banking, and how for decades in Europe diamond money has made people wealthy.

It will tell you the history of diamonds and their use as money since long before the time of Christ.

This book will show you how to grow rich with diamonds. I know, because my family did it. What is more, out of the hundreds of millions of dollars in diamonds I have personally helped to sell, I have never, *not once*, seen anyone who held their stones for the minimum investment period lose money.

If you have wondered about the true value of the diamonds you have, if you are looking for a safe haven in our inflation-ridden economy, if you want to make an honest and substantial profit (after taxes, after inflation), this book is for you.

CHAPTER ONE

Diamonds—
The Best Insurance

F inancial security is at the heart of every investment decision the ordinary person makes, and in recent years we have seen many of the supposedly secure investment options behave in a very unpredictable way. Common stocks, bonds, mutual funds, real estate, gold and silver have all lost the allure they once had, as inflation and other factors caused their values to fluctuate wildly or fall off alarmingly. There is really only one investment that has continued to behave predictably and positively, and that is diamonds.

Everyone knows that diamonds have gone up in value, but few people know just how much. The chart on the next page, Figure 1–1, gives a very rough approximation of the appreciation of investment-quality diamonds (which represent about two percent of all diamonds). Unlike those for nearly any other commodity, this chart shows an overall trend that goes steadily upward. But a chart is a cold and impersonal method of gauging what diamonds have done. I have seen the results of diamond investing on a far more personal level.

A True Diamond Story

Every Christmas my family and I go to Mt. Rose, Colorado, a little town of about a thousand people on the western side of the Rockies, to have dinner with literally hundreds of friends. Last

Figure 1–1

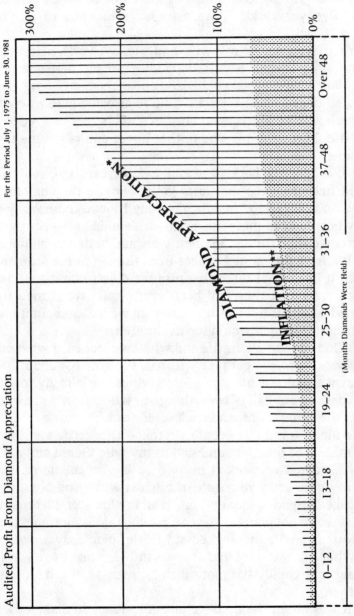

Audited Profit From Diamond Appreciation

For the Period July 1, 1975 to June 30, 1981

300%

200%

100%

0%

*DIAMOND APPRECIATION

**INFLATION

0–12   13–18   19–24   25–30   31–36   37–48   Over 48

(Months Diamonds Were Held)

* Data based on CPA audit of IDC Gemstone Brokerage Service liquidations during the period July 1, 1975 to June 30, 1981

** Accumulated Inflation during the period July 1, 1975 to June 30, 1981 based on increases in Consumer Price Index.

5

year after the dinner a man rose to his feet. He was gaunt-looking and gruff-voiced, a man of the earth who was perhaps seventy-five years old. "I want to say something to all you folks," he began.

"Most of you know my wife and me. We've lived on this mountain all our lives. My Granddaddy came out here in a covered wagon. He homestaked the land and etched out a farm after he cleared the rocks. There wasn't a tree growing here when he built the house in which I was born. It's still here. I've lived in it all my life. I brought my wife to that house and raised my two girls there.

"Well, when my back gave out a few years ago, my girls couldn't help me keep that farm going because they had both married and moved to Phoenix. One day I found there was just no way I could keep that farm. So my wife and I took a square of land that we thought had the best view and built a small house there. We took the money we got from the rest of the farm and invested it in mutual funds, because we didn't know anything else and we heard they had been pretty safe. We trusted the people who told us to buy, so we took all we had and put it into those funds, hoping it would see us through.

"But God gave us a long life and when we looked at what our money was doing we got pretty scared. We saw that about half of what we had put up in our life savings was already lost or gone. That's about half of everything our whole family had built up over the generations, and we lost it so quick!

"One night—and I'll never forget this—I got up on my elbow in the middle of the night and said to my wife 'Here I am, a bib overall farmer. I've worked my whole life on this farm. I've raised my girls and I've got them hitched with good boys. I've never asked anybody for anything in all my life. But, I'll be gone to hell if we're not going to have to ask those kids for some help, and soon.' My wife just looked at me and didn't say a word. I knew what she was thinking. She was thinking that there wasn't anything that could take more dignity away from a man than doing that.

"That was about the time we put our money in diamonds. It was a few years ago. Now, I'm standing up here today because I

6

want to tell you what diamonds have done for me. They have made it possible for us not to have to ask our kids to help us out."

When that man finished talking, there were people with tears in their eyes, and I was one of them. I think this story is worth retelling because it illustrates the true value of diamonds. Even when times get hard, they can still deliver a life with dignity—a life of financial freedom.

Perhaps you know of similar situations. I certainly do. I have seen the value of diamonds up close. After a terrible financial turnaround in which I lost very nearly everything, diamonds pulled me back into the world of financial independence.

What Diamonds Did for Me

To understand my relationship with diamonds, you need to know how I got started in business. I didn't follow the usual teenage pattern. While others were finishing high school I took it into my head to go out into the business world. I had the boldness to begin forming companies and the good fortune to have several of them succeed. One, the Coral Garden Development Company, was formed to build a major resort hotel on the island of Tahiti in French Polynesia; eventually the TraveLodge of Australia built there.

The success of my companies gave me the money and freedom to travel, and one day I was introduced to an old banker in Switzerland. He showed me that Europeans did not bank simply in dollars or francs or deutsche marks. They also banked in gold, silver, and the queen of monies, diamonds. It was a revelation to me that diamond banking was possible. It was a concept that stuck with me and I determined to bring it back to this country.

By the time I was twenty-three years old, I had a number of firms in various stages of promotion and success. These included a film finance company that handled major Hollywood productions, an entertainment management firm that handled popular singing groups, and a railroad tankcar investment company. But I had not forgotten the idea of diamond banking, and was just then planting the seeds for a diamond investment company. I had had the good fortune to meet Steve Greenbaum, one of the world's great diamond experts, who was then operating his own diamond evaluation laboratory. Steve knew diamonds and I knew diamond banking, so we joined together to bring the European idea of diamonds to America. The future seemed bright and unclouded.

Then, in 1973, I discovered that in one of the companies I owned, U. S. Tankcars, certain funds had been misdirected in what was then a public offering regulated by the federal government. The activity was illegal. I assumed full responsibility as an officer and director of the firm. Eventually it was fully established and proven to the satisfaction of everyone including the government that I had not taken any money personally nor in any way profited personally from what happened. However, because I tried initially to correct the problem without immediately notifying authorities, I was at fault. I pled guilty to one infraction of Security and Exchange Commission law. As a result, I lost everything I had built, including all of my companies.

However, my family, Steve Greenbaum, and numerous other friends stood by me. I went back to the fledgling diamond business and, with the aid of Steve and my family, bought diamonds in Europe and sold them to U.S. investors. The company prospered and soon became the largest diamonds investment firm in the world, International Diamond Corporation, doing well over $100 million a year in business.

I have seen diamonds bring thousands of people a sense of financial freedom. I believe they can do the same for you. I've traveled throughout the world. I talk regularly with bankers and political leaders of the major industrial nations. I frequently visit England, Israel, Belgium, France and many other countries, and I conclude that diamonds offer the safest, the truest, the easiest method of generating or preserving wealth.

Security in a Changing World

Few of you will choose to make the diamond business your life work, as I have done, but that will not prevent you from having the security that diamonds can provide.

Do you feel safe today? Most of us don't like to think about this, but I believe that in the corner of everyone's mind there lurks the fear that the economic and social world we operate in today might suddenly change. There are certainly many signs that drastic changes are likely and may be imminent.

ISLAND AMERICA

The typical American has little interest in what is happening outside the United States. We like to be cozy in our own small "island" on this planet. Our concerns tend to be local and even frivolous. We have a tizzy if we get in the car, turn the key and it doesn't start. Judging by our commercials, what truly makes us happy is a Big Mac, a cola and some french fries. Our generation has inherited a tradition of self-indulgence.

Other nations are watching as we continue to indulge our taste for luxury while people in other parts of the world are barely surviving. Regardless of how tough we Americans think we have it in the face of inflation and other internal problems, others see that we are still a thousand times better off than they are. I think it is time to take a realistic look at the major problems that may pose a threat to the United States from without.

FOOD AND ENERGY CRISES

When we hear of the energy crisis, we tend to think of not getting gas for our cars. But for most of the world energy means fertilizer and pesticides. Both of these are products of oil. I would guess that, without fertilizer and pesticides, perhaps 50 percent of all the crops in the world would fail. In recent years, there have been significant crop failures in Russia. They have necessitated purchases of food from other countries, such as the sale of grain to Russia that caused so much controversy in this country a few years ago. The same thing is happening in China. In Africa people are starving by the millions every year. Yet most of us are barely aware of this.

Back in 1976 the CIA reported that the Russians would be short of oil by the 1980s, and this is apparently happening. Their old oil fields are drying up and they are having increasing difficulty in developing new oil fields in their harsh northern areas.

For the Russians this does not mean one less trip to the grocery store in the family car. It means an increased pressure on food because of potential restrictions in fertilizers and pesticides. This oil shortage affects not just Russia, but all its Eastern European satellite countries. The result has been unrest on the Soviet Union's western borders as problems grow in countries such as Poland and Czechoslovakia. Is it any wonder that Russia is massing troops close to the oil-rich Middle Eastern countries?

IS WAR LIKELY?

Americans have always assured themselves that all-out war is unthinkable because of the possibility of nuclear holocaust. Perhaps so, but the history of the human race shows us that all weapons, once invented, have eventually been used. When the crossbow was invented it was banned at first, but later became common. Dynamite was discovered by Alfred Bernhard Nobel, who apparently felt that using it would make war unimaginable. As the story goes, when Nobel found that it only made war more horrible, he devoted all the money from his discovery to the Nobel prizes, most important of which was the peace prize.

Since nuclear bombs were used in 1945, and justified on the basis that American lives would be saved, it is not impossible to imagine a day when some equally compelling justification might finally find acceptance. Would we not justify its use again if the Russians, spurred by their own hunger, moved into the Middle East?

Even if you don't believe this scenario is possible, let alone probable, I think it does give us some reason for thinking about things we don't usually like to think about. It does bring to mind the real problems of energy and food that are facing the world and tends to put aside the frivolous concerns of a Big Mac generation. At the very least, the next few years are a period of great danger and vulnerability. There is every justification for thinking of ways to provide as much security as possible for ourselves and our families.

NON-NUCLEAR EMERGENCIES

Quite apart from the threat of war, a state of emergency could

10

arise as the result of energy shortages or natural disasters. What if there were no longer heat in our homes? What if we couldn't preserve foods because there were no electricity for our refrigerators? What if there were no light? Perhaps we'd use firewood and candles. Yet most people have no access to trees and not everyone has a fireplace, and if a hundred million people started buying candles all at once it would be pretty hard to find them. But food, heat and light could be bought *somehow* if we had something valuable and portable to use as a medium of exchange.

A "God Forbid" Account

Every sane person must at least consider the possibility of disaster. Prudent people usually make some kind of preparation for such unpredictable events—the kind you only mention along with the words "God forbid." In my family we have always had a special account that is set aside for just such emergencies, and we have always called it our "God forbid" account. We will only use it if what we don't want to think about actually comes to pass.

Our God forbid account contains nothing but diamonds. You are probably thinking of the traditional investing advice that diversification is the best way to protect your interests for the future. But let me tell you what happened in Viet Nam at the end of the war. Of course it was plain to the leaders of South Viet Nam that the United States was not willing to throw its entire military weight into the war as it had done during the Second World War. If we had once more been willing to pay the price in men lost and resources spent, we could have done it, but the American people were divided and a no-win situation came about.

Both President Tu and Vice-President Kee realized that some day the U.S. would pull out, and then it would only be a matter of time until the North prevailed. So both leaders put aside something for the day when their entire lives might crumble around them.

Everyone thought President Tu was very smart. He bought

gold. The reports I have seen indicate he had something like $17 million in gold bars stuffed in vaults in his palace. When the end came he tried to take it with him, but he couldn't get it out! It was simply too heavy. In the confusion and rioting at the end, he was unable to get helicopters to transport his personal fortune.

Vice-President Kee had no gold at all. His family had diamonds. He came to the United States with diamonds hidden in hatbands and babies' diapers. He sold some of his diamonds, and today he has his relatives staying at the best hotels in Mexico. The diamonds in his God forbid account transferred his wealth— his ability to survive economically—out of the holocaust of Saigon and into a new life and new opportunity elsewhere.

The Diamond Solution

Vice-President Kee's story is not unique. Down through history diamonds have always been the money of last resort—not gold, as most people have believed. Gold would not feed the German people after the First World War when currency was worthless. People had tampered with gold. They had melted it down and added base metals. Since gold could be tampered with, no one would trust it.

Diamonds are recognized as valuable by everyone. Can you imagine showing a beautiful, glistening diamond to anyone and not having them instantly recognize it as wealth? And, as Vice-President Kee found out, they are truly portable. Try getting a bar of gold past an X-ray detection machine at an airport and see how far you get. Yet you could have a pocket full of diamonds, a million dollars in wealth, and never be stopped. Even today, when nearly every country in the world restricts the amount of cash or gold that can be brought across the borders without declaration, diamonds still pass *legally* from country to country. Millions of dollars in the form of diamonds cross borders without question.

I have a friend from Germany who told me how life was just after World War II. One beautiful day she went for a picnic with some wealthy friends. That day marked the end of the old Germany and the beginning of a new world for them. All economic differences had been washed away by the defeat. Now they were equal. In effect they would go home from that picnic and the government would give each of them twenty-five dollars to start over. No matter what each person had been worth before, now they were all worth $25.

Except for those who had saved diamonds. My friend told me how difficult life was for her and how incredibly easy it was for those who had diamonds. Within weeks they were financially healthy again. They didn't starve, they didn't go without clothes or shelter. Nor did their children.

Of course, it won't happen here in the United States. It couldn't, could it? Well, I have met many people who have lived through great disasters, and they don't think it is impossible. Even if it *is* next to impossible, don't you think you should at least consider a God forbid account? The worst you could do is make what will probably be the best investment of your life.

Diamonds as an Investment

To see what I mean, let's compare the appreciation of diamonds with inflation. Our money is worth less and less. But just for a moment let's consider a different kind of money—diamond money. Suppose you bought a single diamond back in 1950. We will assume it weighed one carat, had perfect color, was flawless and an excellent cut. Chances are you would have paid $500 for that stone. Now let's follow that stone and see what the price appreciation was at five-year intervals:

1950	$ 500
1955	850
1960	1,000
1965	1,500
1970	2,200
1975	8,000
1980	45,000
1985	75,000 (est.)

(Note: Each diamond is unique, so the pricing here is just an approximation.)

As you can see, the diamond's value would have increased

substantially between 1970 and 1975 and dramatically just prior to 1980, when having good color became especially desirable. At any point along the way, the diamond would have been worth far more than you paid.

Just think what that means. During the same thirty-five years that saw paper money become worth less and less, our diamond increased in value some 9000 percent, which was more than twenty times the rate of inflation! If we had chosen to buy diamond money back in 1950 instead of dealing in paper money, think where we would be today.

The same holds true for the future. I believe the diamond prices we see today are just the tip of the iceberg. In fact, I think today's prices are bargains. A high-quality half-carat stone may be worth $2000 or $3000 today, but in just a few years it could be worth $15,000 to $20,000. A one-carat stone of lesser quality that sells for what people think is an incredible price today—$10,000 to $20,000—will seem cheap when in the future it sells for $250,000.

Of course, it's not necessary to buy these particular weights of diamonds. *All* diamonds in investment grades appreciate in value, including those available for just a few hundred dollars today. The point is that it is not too late to buy. The train hasn't left. There is still time to get a ticket and grow rich with diamonds!

As I mentioned in the Preface, I have helped to sell hundreds of millions of dollars worth of diamonds over the past few years. Yet I don't know of a single person who kept the diamonds at least thirty-six months (the minimum investment period) who did not show a profit of some kind. That includes every grade and every weight, and there are thousands of different grades and weights. (*Note:* The 36-month minimum waiting period is not arbitrary. As we will see when we discuss the DeBeers syndicate, it is carefully planned.)

I believe totally, passionately, in diamonds. I know what they have done for my family. I have seen what they have done for others. Through this book I hope to show what they can do for you.

CHAPTER TWO

Diamonds and Inflation

M ost people find economics a difficult subject. I think this is because economists seem to look for esoteric reasons to explain events long after the fact. In addition, they tend to interpret developments impersonally. Since many of them do not have the opportunity of knowing the personalities that shape world events, they concentrate on trends and mass movements without understanding the deeply personal human motivations that contribute to them.

I am not out to knock economists, but I have my own perspective on what's happening in the world today. It comes from traveling extensively and talking with world leaders in finance and politics. My own world economic view is that, today, buying diamonds is not merely an option to be compared with buying stocks, bonds, gold, silver, real estate, or whatever else you can name. *Buying diamonds is the only option. There is no other.*

Paper Money

There is a television commercial that never ceases to make me chuckle. Perhaps you have seen it. A man, apparently a banker, is standing behind a stack of bills while saying something like "Money doesn't grow on trees." He goes on to say that if you put your money in his institution it is guaranteed up to $100,000. The implication is that no matter what happens—if there is a war, if there is a run on the bank—you can always come and get your money.

Well, money may not *grow* on trees, but it comes from trees. Trees are cut down to make the paper on which money is printed, and we will never run out of paper money so long as there are trees. Of course it's guaranteed—it's only paper! The printing presses can run at full speed twenty-four hours a day and fulfill the demands of every depositor in the country. The real question for any thinking person has got to be "What is that paper money worth?"

As we have all seen during our lifetime, that paper is worth less and less each year. When we go to the stores to buy food, clothing, a car, or even a few nuts and bolts to do simple home repairs, we are amazed at how many of those paper dollars it takes to buy what we want, at least when compared to how many it took only a few years ago. We are the front-line soldiers when it comes to inflation. I don't have to tell you about it and you don't have to tell me. We are all out in the trenches fighting inflation on a day-by-day basis.

Permanent Inflation

The inflation economy that we have now is permanent. The present inflation got its start when the government began debasing currency. Inflation surged during the Second World War, moved upward slowly during the 1950s, and then exploded with a vengeance from about 1966 onward. Since that time the rate of acceleration has been steadily increasing and our government has been helpless to do anything about it.

Most people believe the President came into office promising to halt inflation. That's not the case. What he actually said was that he would bring inflation under control. He said, in effect, that this "car" called "inflation" is going down the road at 10 miles an hour. It appears that next year the car will be going down the road at 25 miles an hour and the year after that it will be 50. He never said he would stop the car or put it into reverse. He never even said he would slow the car. Rather, he promised to *slow the speed of acceleration*.

He was only being honest. The inflation we have seen thus far

16

will be dwarfed by the inflation in our future, looking ahead to the mid-1980s. The rate may be slowed momentarily. But, over-all, inflation is going to get worse. I see a 35 percent inflation rate for this country before the decade is out. It will probably occur by 1985.

But why is inflation inevitable? We got along during the 1950s without much inflation. It was down around 5 percent when President Ford left office. Why won't it drop again? Inflation does go down, but only on a *short-term* basis. Looking at it month by month we can sometimes see a drop. The inflation rate as reported by the government's Consumer Price Index (CPI)—an almost worthless figure when it comes to practical application but one upon which we can all usually agree—was down near zero during the summer months of 1980. Yet inflation for the year as a whole was close to 13 percent. It's in the big picture that inflation really shows.

The inflation rate for a given year may also have been down to 2 to 4 percent back in the 1960s and 1970s. But, if we look at five-year periods, we see that it has gone upward at an accelerating rate. In five-year periods, even going back as far as the Second World War, inflation has been steadily up, never down.

Of course, we have only discussed inflation from the view-point of how it has done in the past. We must also consider why it has occurred in the past and what that portends for the future.

How Inflation Begins

Inflation comes about when we print money that has no real value. Value is not an intrinsic part of money. This is most easily seen by looking at a primitive society where money does not yet exist, and barter is the rule. To barter something, it must fulfill two requirements: It must be useful, such as food or clothing, and it must be scarce. (No one will barter air, for example, since it exists everywhere.)

In our primitive society Peter wants to hunt deer for food. He fashions a bow and arrow and becomes a hunter. John has found a dead bear. He skins the animal and makes the skin into a robe. John now has a robe, and Peter has food. It turns out that

Peter is cold after his hunt and would like the robe. John, on the other hand, is hungry. They barter their two valued items and an exchange is made.

How did the two items gain their value? In part, it was always there in the deer and the bear. But in part the value came from labor: Peter's stalking and killing the deer, John's finding and skinning the bear. Value came both from work and from natural resources.

But John and Peter's simple society could not last long. How could John barter for one steak instead of an entire deer? How could Peter barter for just a vest instead of the whole bearskin robe? In bartering, it's very difficult to make fractions come out even. And there's also the problem of lugging around both the robe and the deer meat. The obvious solution is a *medium of exchange*, which eventually becomes known as *money*.

MONEY AS DESIGNATED BUYING POWER

Money solves many of the problems of the barter. If Peter and John designate that a bearskin robe is worth one ounce of gold and a side of deer meat is also worth one ounce of gold, then fractional exchanges become easy. A steak might be worth one-tenth of an ounce, but it would not be necessary for John to cut his robe into tenths to buy the steak. All he would need is one-tenth of an ounce of gold. Similarly, a vest might be worth half an ounce. Peter wouldn't have to cut his deer meat in half if he had half an ounce of gold. In addition, neither would need to carry all their goods around. A few ounces of gold in a bag would handle it all.

Money becomes the vehicle for the exchange. In this case, the money happens to be gold. Note that the gold money does not have value itself. The value resides in the bearskin robe and in the deer meat. Whether the money were clam shells or shiny rocks, it by itself would have no value. Only when it has *designated buying power* do people want it.

Not everything will work as money. Common rocks would not do. For money to work it has to be *scarce*. This is one reason why gold, silver and diamonds were early choices.

You might think it is simple to have money as the medium for exchange. But as soon as money gets designated, problems arise.

18

The problems come from the amount of money that is available. If gold is the designated money, and one ounce is given the value of a skin robe and one ounce a side of deer meat, what happens when a new gold mine is found? If the supply of gold suddenly increases, then its value as a medium of exchange diminishes. In this lies the heart of inflation. *Money only works when it is scarce.*

EXPANDING THE MONEY SUPPLY

Money can be like a two-edged sword. Too much is not good, but neither is too little. For example, if there are only four robes and four sides of meat exchanged a month, perhaps a handful of gold pieces will do. Any more would be inflationary. But if there were forty million robes and ten million sides of meat, would a handful of coins suffice? Of course not. We would need truckloads of gold.

Yet this would not necessarily be inflationary. As long as the amount of gold and the amount of goods or services retained the original ratio (one ounce for each item), no inflation would take place. The supply of money would merely have been expanded to accomodate increased economic activity.

This is why those who advocate returning to a gold standard are wrong. The supply of gold is relatively inflexible. While it would certainly restrain inflation (since an overabundance could not be produced, it would remain scarce), it would also restrain economic growth (since the money supply could not grow to accommodate more people and more products).

WHY GOVERNMENTS CHOOSE PAPER MONEY

Ultimately, the choice of money made by virtually all governments is paper. The reason is simple. The government has complete control over the supply. It can chop down trees and print as much or as little as it desires.

When a government is careful and honest, it only prints enough money to accommodate the amount of economic activity that exists. No inflation occurs. But when a government is lax and dishonest, it tends to print more money than is justified. (The temptation to be dishonest is great. After all, the government gets to spend the excess initially.)

This tendency to print more money than is justified seems

ever-present. The government always wants to spend more money than it receives in taxes. Somehow the income from taxes and other sources never quite covers the desired expenditures for social welfare, defense and other programs.

The National Debt—
Our Inflationary Millstone

During the 1860s, when President Lincoln was having trouble raising funds to fight the Civil War, the government simply printed "greenback" dollars. There was nothing scarce about them. Almost immediately greenbacks became inflated, worthless paper. Today, although the printing of currency is growing by an enormous amount each year, the government uses a more sophisticated system involving the Federal Reserve and banks across the country. Put simply, the government borrows. It creates a national debt.

The national debt, when last I looked, was more than $1 trillion. Think of it! That figure is almost incomprehensible. It could be written another way: 1,000 billion dollars. That's how much the federal government has borrowed. Now comes the rub. There is interest to be paid on that national debt.

In years past, when interest rates were relatively low, the government was able to borrow new money to cover old debt fairly easily. At a rate of only 4% a year, the interest on $1000 billion comes to about $40 billion. But when interest rates jumped, the government found it was refinancing that debt at rates of 15% and higher. At a rate of 15%, the interest on $1000 billion comes to a whopping $150 billion. That is equivalent to $45,000 over the lifetime of every man, woman and child in the United States. Keep in mind that this $150 billion includes not a single dollar towards repayment of the debt. Adding to this the overspending that the government is continuing to do, some $50 billion or more per year in expenditures over income, we see that there is an enormous amount of extra money the government has to come up with. Where does the government get it? The actual process is fairly complicated and involves banks, the Federal Reserve and the Bureau of Engraving and Printing. But the ultimate answer is that it simply chops down more trees and prints more money.

But, as we saw, the value of money comes from its scarcity. When it stops being scarce, its designated buying power changes. When gold becomes plentiful, it soon takes more than one gold piece to buy a robe or a side of meat. By creating money over and above the amount that can be absorbed by growth of the economy, the government has made that money worth less in terms of real buying power. The government has created the beast of inflation.

ANTICIPATION OF INFLATION

As if inflation weren't bad enough, it has a sidekick that always seems to tag along—anticipation. We have all come to expect things to be higher priced tomorrow than they are today. Therefore, we all spend the money we have today as quickly as possible before its buying power diminishes. We don't save our money—we spend it. We even *borrow* to spend, hoping to pay back our debt tomorrow with cheaper dollars.

The result of all this is an enormous increase in the money supply, an increase above and beyond the amount increased by the federal government. When the public anticipates inflation, it actually creates more inflation!

Why the Government Can't Control Inflation

Inflation is stopped by controlling the money supply. Reducing the amount of money in circulation will have the opposite effect of increasing it. It will bring inflation down. The problem, in my opinion, is that the government has no idea what the true money supply is. The Federal Reserve supposedly keeps track of the money supply in the United States. Through its various ratings (M1A, M1B, M2, M3) and other so-called sophisticated measurements, it keeps track of money in savings accounts, checking accounts, NOW accounts, and so forth. This it calls the money supply.

21

But this measurement is archaic and the calculations—as a means of looking at what is really happening to money in the economy—are ridiculous. The simple fact is that in our society today the true money supply is composed of all the *credit* available and no one, but no one, has any idea how much that is!

That is why the government's attempts to control inflation are feeble and doomed to failure. How can it ever hope to control something it can't even measure?

What the Future Holds

When I try to put it all together, I come up with two forces hammering against each other. On the one hand we have government's insatiable desire to spend more than it takes in, even under conservative administrations. On the other hand we have government's inability to come to terms with controlling the money supply. The only result there can possibly be is *more inflation*. In the short run perhaps inflation will be temporarily reduced, but in the long run a steady acceleration of devalued paper money is inevitable.

What Do We Do About It?

The answer that most people found a decade ago was to invest in "hard" commodities such as gold, silver and diamonds. These items, because they were limited in supply, tended to retain their value. (Because of demand, in many cases these items momentarily increased even beyond the rate of inflation.) Diamonds used to be one of the most important and viable of these options. But not any more.

Today diamonds are the only viable option. They are the ultimate. They are so far ahead of anything else that the difference is astonishing to anyone who understands them. Let's consider some of the alternatives.

GOLD AND SILVER
Many people have invested in gold and silver. They put all their

excess assets in these two commodities, hoping to avoid the calamities of inflation. But nothing could be a worse choice. Gold and silver today are speculative assets. They have been destabilized. Individuals buy and sell them. Large corporations buy and sell them. Governments trade in gold and to some degree in silver. The result is that speculators control and influence the precious metals.

There is no longer any relationship between price and what it costs to mine and distribute gold and silver. It's all a game. Gold can soar from $300 to nearly $900 an ounce within just a few months, then plummet to $500, then move all over the charts. What kind of protection from inflation is that? If you were to buy high and then have to sell low, you could have an enormous portion of your money wiped out. That's not safety, that's risk— high risk—and silver is even worse.

Silver can be $46 an ounce one day and $11 a few days later. Where is the relation between the real cost of silver and the market price? Where is the supply-and-demand balance? It's not there because silver, like gold, is speculative money. Both are simply gaming tokens in a worldwide game of chance. You put your money down and you take your chance. Maybe you win, maybe you don't. But certainly under no realistic definition have you made an *investment* when you buy gold and silver. (And what happens if the gold or silver you bought in good faith turns out to have been debased or alloyed with a cheap metal?)

MUTUAL FUNDS

I like to categorize stocks and bonds under mutual funds because in the past that is the way most people have invested in them. For those who put their money in mutual funds, there's really very little I can say. You put your money in, I presume you lost it (in terms of inflation-adjusted dollars), and now you're looking for something else.

Mutual funds have been inflation negative. By that I mean that they have been no better than savings accounts in banks. While it is true that those who put money in generally get more dollars when they take it out, in virtually every case I've seen, after tax and inflation the net result was a loss, not a gain.

CURRENCY

Some bolder investors have bought currency itself. This to me is the height of speculation. In our example of bartering, we saw that currency has no intrinsic value. It should represent value for goods and services. But "investing" in currency presumes that the money itself has some sort of intrinsic value—the money becomes a commodity.

The true commodity value of money is the value of the paper it is printed on—perhaps one thousandth of a cent per sheet. We see this demonstrated constantly in the money marketplace. One day a particular currency is up in relation to other currencies and the next day it is down. I can think of no better example than the Swiss franc.

For years the Swiss franc was the darling of investors. People bought Swiss francs and saw them rise in value relative to other currencies. It happened for many years in a row and people became convinced that the Swiss franc was a true commodity that was inflation positive. Every professional person in the United States seemed to have a Swiss bank account. The Arabs had so much money in Swiss banks that even the Swiss must have had trouble counting it!

But consider: How many people are there in Switzerland? The answer is seven million, less than in Los Angeles County. How can a population of seven million people control an economy of billions and billions and billions of Swiss francs? An economy where the rich and wealthy of the world keep buying their currency?

The answer is that they print more francs. Just as in the United States, the Swiss print more and more of their currency to accommodate the need for it. Why, there's hardly a tree left standing in Switzerland for all the francs they've printed! Seriously, to accommodate the demand they have had to inflate their economy enormously. Yet paradoxically the Swiss have reported one of the lowest inflation rates in the world. How come?

For a good many years the Swiss kept their francs at home. People bought Swiss francs and then kept them on deposit in Swiss banks. That was the secret. The money never left the country. But when in the 1980s the interest rates in the United

States rose enormously, suddenly those who owned Swiss francs began to think that putting their money in dollars made more sense. So they sold the Swiss francs and invested in the U.S. and in Britain, which also had high interest rates, and elsewhere.

As an investment against inflation, the Swiss franc suddenly couldn't tow the line. It sank. Once again I have to ask what kind of protection against inflation is an investment that at some point may go down in value?

REAL ESTATE

In recent years real estate has been seen as the prime investment hedge in the United States. The price of property soared year after year and people put their life savings into real estate. But is it really all it is cracked up to be?

Real estate has indeed gone up in value by leaps and bounds. But why has it gone up? Some experts point to a supply-and-demand situation: There simply have not been enough homes and other types of property to meet the demand. I'm sure that is true. But I'm equally sure that short supply has not caused the incredible prices. The reason real estate went up between 1975 and 1979 was *financing*.

The financing of real estate was born during the Great Depression. At that time loans of thirty years' duration became customary so that families could buy homes they otherwise would be unable to afford. Thirty-year loans were the rule right up until this decade. As long as lenders felt reasonably confident they could do better than the inflation rate, they made loans. To assure this, interest rates gradually rose. Few people recall that in the 1940s, 4% real-estate loans were common. Rates moved to 6% in the 1950s and 8% in the 1960s. Inflation was a fact of life and interest rates on mortgages rose accordingly.

But in the 1970s, inflation began to accelerate and so did interest rates. By the end of the last decade the rates were up to 12%. Still the lenders could handle it. Then inflation moved ahead. According to the Consumer Price Index, inflation was between 12% and 13% during 1979 and 1980.

Perhaps it was and perhaps it wasn't. The Consumer Price Index includes almost every kind of item you could name; it includes interest rates and rents and soap and clothespins and perhaps a hundred items that most of us never buy. Just going shopping tells me that inflation on items such as food and clothing must be a lot worse than the government is saying.

In any event, lenders began to see the handwriting on the wall. They saw that inflation was out of control and accelerating and they saw something else: They could no longer afford to be tied into thirty-year loans. They couldn't possibly set an interest rate today that would be inflation positive for thirty years in the future—not when they didn't know where inflation and interest rates were going to be next month!

So the old thirty-year mortgage went out the door and in its place we have the "rollover." The rollover is a loan whose interest rate is renegotiated after a specified period of time. In talking with presidents of banks, I have come to the conclusion that the *only* loan that will soon be available for real estate will be the rollover. According to these lenders, while the rollover term may now be five years, in a few years it will be shortened to two or three and most lenders by 1985 want to see the rollover for a maximum of only one year!

Think what that means. When you buy a piece of real estate, you will only be guaranteed an interest rate for one year. After that it could jump, perhaps 5%! You will have to come up with the money, or sell the house, or lose it.

Suddenly real estate is not nearly as attractive. Remember, almost no one paid cash for property in the past. Most of it was mortgaged, up to 100% of the value. But when mortgages become unattractive and interest rates price out buyers, how can real-estate prices advance? The answer is that they won't. The interest rates may never come down. In any event, during the decade of the 1980s real estate will not be inflation positive because it simply won't have the financing.

Diamonds

Diamonds have none of the drawbacks of the other so-called investment opportunities. They are inflation positive, and have

26

been ever since before the Great Depression. Now I want to explain why diamonds will continue to perform well in the future.

Diamonds are essentially a controlled commodity. The DeBeers syndicate is the controlling influence on the diamond market. In fact, DeBeers controls between 85 and 90 percent of the world's diamond market. If they controlled only 25 percent of the market they would be a major influence on price. If they controlled just 60 percent they would be the absolute influence on price. But at more than 80 percent, they simply dominate the field.

To understand how DeBeers can do this, you must be aware of the size of the syndicate. DeBeers, with its parent Anglo-American Corporation, rivals all but a few world governments in its assets. Note that I said *governments*. It far exceeds in size what we have come to think of as a powerful multinational company. Some estimates indicate that DeBeers has capital reserves of approximately $4 billion. That is 4000 million dollars. These funds are available to support the diamond market if the need arises.

It would be a misconception, however, to think that DeBeers ordinarily *supports* the price of diamonds. To the contrary, DeBeers acts to *steady* the price of diamonds so that the price moves upward, not by leaps and bounds, but gradually and persistently. To maintain this steady price rise, DeBeers has generally acted, not to support prices, but to keep them down! These slow price rises have kept speculators out of the diamond market and given it a fundamental stability unlike any other.

For the ordinary diamond buyer as well as the serious investor the presence of DeBeers has been beneficial. In recent years diamonds have accelerated at a steady rate that is greater than the rate of inflation. There have been no explosions in price, but there have been no plunges either. For the future, with DeBeers in control we can expect more of the same.

But what if DeBeers were to collapse or be wrenched aside, leaving the diamond market open? I cannot think of anything more profitable for those who had already invested in diamonds.

We would see sudden sensational profits before the cycles began in the marketplace. Those who bought beforehand would do very well indeed, as they saw their investments soar in price.

Of course, I don't anticipate there is the slightest chance that will happen. Rather I see diamonds as being inflation positive for an indefinite time into the future. I can foresee no time when investment-quality stones would not increase in value, except in the event of a worldwide depression such as the Great Depression of the 1930s. Even then, if we consider precedent, diamonds should continue to outperform other investments.

Diamond Investors Today

Another aspect of diamonds has to do with who is buying. For hundreds of years diamonds have been bought by wealthy individuals. They have been bought as an expression of wealth, as a God forbid account and, more recently, as an inflation hedge. But you don't have to be a millionaire to own diamonds today. There is approximately $1.6 trillion in bank accounts making a negative return against inflation. There are hundreds of billions of dollars more in savings and loan associations, mutual funds and other paper instruments. All of these tend to make a negative return against inflation. Over 127,000,000 Americans are holding their capital reserves in these losers while they seek a better alternative. Diamonds are that better alternative.

This new diamond alternative is just being discovered by many Americans. If only a fraction of them buy, using only a fraction of their capital reserves, we could very quickly see them purchase every diamond ever mined.

This discovery of diamonds by the American public has not been unobserved. Pension funds in the United States, oil-rich Middle Eastern countries and the great banks of the world have been watching the phenomenon closely. And recently they have quietly begun buying diamonds. Apparently they have learned that the time to purchase is before the rush.

With new small investors and new giant investors coming into the field, we have the makings of a different and greatly expanded world of diamond investing. The current market, it could very well turn out, is nothing more than the tip of the iceberg.

CHAPTER THREE

DeBeers—
The Benevolent Giant

Many people have mixed feelings about the name DeBeers. For them it comes too close to being Big Brother. At best, they would say, it is an uncontrollable cartel, stockpiling great numbers of diamonds so that market prices are artificially high; at worst, it is a malignant dabbler in the internal affairs of national governments. I see neither of these things in the DeBeers syndicate.

In DeBeers I see a giant, but a benevolent one. The DeBeers syndicate does take actions which affect everyone in the diamond business, but from my own personal experience I can say that inevitably these actions are beneficial, not harmful, to everyone involved.

To begin to understand DeBeers, you must first get some idea of the organization's size and power. Then we can better examine its pricing policies and their effects.

The Rise of DeBeers

The history of the modern DeBeers syndicate began after the First World War, with a man named Sir Ernest Oppenheimer. It was a period of great disruptions in the diamond trade. New and fabulously rich diamond mines were being discovered. These discoveries started an incredible diamond rush at a time of slack demand. Miners sold their diamond shares without much concern for the stability of the market. The DeBeers syndicate, the only centralized diamond trading organization at the time, handled only a small part of world production. It was virtually impossible for the syndicate to keep prices stable.

And then along came Oppenheimer, a man of vision and daring. In the years after the First World War, Oppenheimer had gained control of 20 percent of African production of rough diamonds. In 1926 he joined the board of directors of DeBeers; three years later he became its chairman.

Oppenheimer understood clearly that, in order to control diamond prices effectively, one single organization would have to buy most of the diamonds from the major world producers. To accomplish that, he centralized diamond purchasing and diamond sales within one firm—DeBeers. The system Oppenheimer established gave DeBeers the lion's share of the diamond market, and control over the pricing policies of the market at large. As a result, DeBeers was able to stabilize and protect prices, even during the disastrous economic depression of the 1930's. That system of control remains basically unchanged today.

DeBeers Is Everywhere

Let's assume that you had the great fortune to be planting geraniums in your back yard and discover a diamond there. It is not a diamond someone lost from a ring or a pendant, but a diamond in the rough—the real thing as it occurs in nature. You take it to a gemologist who confirms that it is indeed a diamond. "By the way," he asks, "Where did you find this?"

You decline to answer. Instead you go home, form a corporation of every friend and relative who has money and buy up all the land around your house. You send ore samples to labs and get reports that, yes indeed, you are sitting on what may well be one of the richest deposits of diamond-bearing kimberlite in the world.

"I'm on Easy Street from now on," you think. You go to the bank, tell them what you want, and they sound positive about coming up with financing to develop the mine. You have an organization, you have financing, what more could you want?

You call a meeting of the board of directors, in truth just to congratulate each other on your good fortune. But just as the meeting starts you are suddenly interrupted by a sedate, British-looking gentleman. He apologizes for the interruption, then proceeds to astonish you.

He says he just flew in from London and represents the DeBeers organization. He says his own ore samples from your property confirm your findings. This is a surprise, as you are not a public company and haven't told anyone where the property is, let alone let anyone see ore sample reports.

The British gentleman goes on to say he is fairly sure that your local bank will come up with the $10-million loan for which you applied; in fact, he's just come from the bank president, who was quite optimistic about the project. Unfortunately, developing a diamond mine requires a bit more money, perhaps in the neighborhood of $500 million, and that is where he fits in. The DeBeers organization would like to lend you a benevolent hand.

Several of the board members are quite taken aback and want to throw the gentleman out. However, moderation and common sense prevail and he is allowed to continue.

He says that he can understand their resentment, since his organization has been characterized by some as ruthless. Of course, he points out, that is not the case. He says that DeBeers is a civilized group of individuals who have been doing business for a long time and provide an important service. For example, to open the mine you will need diamond recovery equipment. You will need the special tools used to screen, wash, sort, and recover the diamonds. These include highly sophisticated X-ray and grease separators that get the absolute maximum delivery from ore. He points out that nearly all of this equipment is made by DeBeers subsidiaries or under their parents. You could go into the diamond-mining equipment business as a sideline, but it might be simpler to buy direct.

Then he points out that you will need trained engineers to operate the mine. DeBeers, of course, has a wealth of such specialized people—people with years of experience both in starting up a diamond mine and in fully recovering the diamonds from it.

"Perhaps you've heard what happened in Angola?" He reminds you that the African country of Angola went communist a few years back. Angola is a large producer of diamonds with several mines. One of the first acts of the new communist rulers was to throw out the engineers and managers of the DeBeers organization who were running the mines in Angola. The new Angolans felt they didn't need DeBeers. They could mine the diamonds themselves and get more money. The Angolans felt that DeBeers was putting the diamonds on the market at too low a price. They wanted to mine the diamonds and put them out at a high price.

He pointed out that the reason people want to go around DeBeers is always because they want to make more money. The Angolan communists figured that they could train their own people just as easily as DeBeers could. They would operate for less, and sell for more. Their profit margins would be enormous.

Angola tried it for eighteen months. At the end of that time they had their production up to just 15 percent of what it was before they kicked DeBeers out. And at that point they invited DeBeers back. It took DeBeers an additional eighteen months to get production going well. But by 1980 they had it back to 100 percent of the pre-war level, and it was increasing. The DeBeers group was asked back into Angola while a technical state of war existed between Great Britain and Angola! "Diamonds make for strange bedfellows, don't you agree?" he smiled.

At this point the visitor makes his offer. It essentially is that if you agree to have the new diamond mine join his syndicate then he will agree to buy *all* the diamonds you can produce. He points out that you have a rich mine and you may be turning out a flood of diamonds that could have an adverse affect on world prices. But if you join his group he will guarantee to buy all your diamonds at a price slightly below the world market price. In bad years he will withhold diamonds and in good years he will put them all out. Additionally, every time DeBeers raises the world market price (which it can do because of the quantity of diamonds it controls), he will raise your prices accordingly.

If that arrangement works out satisfactorily at first, eventually a second arrangement may be possible. At that time your mining company can join the Diamond Producers Association. With the DeBeers syndicate they work toward actually setting the world price of diamonds. You will then get full market price, top dollar. But the DeBeers syndicate will have the option of controlling your production. If the market should happen to become soft, you could find your production slightly curtailed.

Either way, the syndicate will assure that you always have enough of a diamond harvest to pay all of your overhead and make a handsome profit. Of course, he would like a shortterm interim agreement while you get to know the DeBeers syndicate and vice versa. Twenty years would do. In the meantime, he is prepared to offer a group financing package that will cover all your costs at about 25 percent below the going interest rate. In addition, he can have engineers on site the following Monday. He also has seventeen oceangoing barges already loaded with equipment and on their way to set up your mine, and scientists and management teams are being flown in from various parts of the globe to get work started. This is all at DeBeers expense. If you don't want it, you don't have to have it and it is his loss. Of course, if you do join the syndicate, he would like to have a bit of the equity of your company—and that would make the financing package even more attractive.

Finally he says that, if you do join, he can guarantee financing, manpower, equipment, and a setup time of 18 to 24 months. If you do it yourselves, the minimum time is usually 11 to 15 years. And, of course, if you go it alone and happen to infringe on any of the DeBeers patents for mining equipment there could be problems. Also, getting insurance on the mining operation is difficult, if not impossible, except through his group.

Would you go for his offer? You bet. It's an offer you couldn't refuse.

Of course this example is strictly hypothetical. I don't know for a fact of any meeting where anything such as this ever happened or even came close to happening. And I seriously doubt whether there is a DeBeers representative such as the man from London whom I have created here.

However, the might of the DeBeers syndicate is not imagined. They do have money, men, technical expertise, equipment, insurance—in effect, an entire package. There are very few who have the desire to go around DeBeers.

The only reason I know of that anyone has ever attempted to go around DeBeers was because they wanted more for their diamonds and felt that DeBeers was keeping the market price too low. The Soviet Union has a kind of contract with DeBeers under which they can sell directly a certain percentage of their crop that they have cut and polished themselves. But they usually charge between 5 and 15 percent more than DeBeers. Do they sell a great deal? Not really. The world market can only absorb so much at the higher price. If they want to unload more, there won't be a market for it. And to sell at the same price as DeBeers makes no sense. They might as well join the syndicate.

The DeBeers organization and its parent Anglo-American Company is so large and has such vast resources, that it simply doesn't make good business sense to deal with anyone but them. They have money, they have position and they have intelligence. (I wouldn't be surprised if they knew about this book the minute I began writing it!) In addition, they make superb policy decisions. Perhaps the most important of these has to do with pricing.

Diamond Pricing

Diamonds have always been a valued possession and investment, and the diamond market even without DeBeers was always strong. However during the Great Depression many, many people lost their money or their jobs and had to make ends meet however they could. This often resulted in selling the family diamonds.

In the early 1930s the diamond market was such that few people felt comfortable making new purchases. Yet thousands were anxious to sell. The result was a decline in diamond prices. Of course, the prices of everything were declining and I believe it is important to note that diamonds' decline was less than that of other items such as stocks or property. Nevertheless, the market became flat and the diamond producers could not sell their new diamonds in such a market.

It was about this time that Sir Ernest Oppenheimer became Chairman of the Board of DeBeers Consolidated Mines. Against the background of the flat market of the Depression, Oppenheimer was able to organize the diamond producers into what is today the DeBeers syndicate.

The policy with regard to pricing that Sir Ernest (and later his son, Harry Oppenheimer) developed and carried out is a policy of stability. Stability means a stable price for diamonds regardless of world conditions. In recessions or even depressions diamond prices would not fall, or fall ever so slightly, and then far less when compared to other investments. On the other hand, in times of prosperity or inflation when demand was great, diamond prices would be held back. The effect would be a flattening out of the great curves of speculation that we see in other investment areas such as gold or stocks. Instead of up-and-down cycles there would be a steady line upward.

In today's economy we see the influence of DeBeers in keeping the price down. At this point I detect a few guffaws from some of my readers. They are saying "Nobody, but nobody, keeps the price *down*. If you want to talk about their stockpiling diamonds to keep the price up, I'll believe you. But, if you want to talk about them selling everything they can get their hands on, dumping diamonds to keep the price down, I can't buy it. It doesn't make sense."

Sending Out False Signals

Yet this is in fact what DeBeers has done. To calm the excitement over diamonds I have heard DeBeers employees off the record (yet fairly loudly!) say they think investing in diamonds is a mistake! They have actually announced to the press that they believe diamonds should be bought for beauty, never as an asset! This is DeBeers publicity. (They have said that they do not think that diamonds can be graded accurately. Yet I believe they hold patents on equipment that would revolutionize grading by using computers and a laser system of identification. But they won't release this kind of system to the market because it would potentially give the speculator a ticker-tape avenue into diamonds. And that is the one thing they dislike the most.)

I have found DeBeers' comments on diamond investment fascinating, particularly since they seem to differ from one side of the Atlantic to the other. In Europe, DeBeers has a Diamond Fellowship program that is almost exclusively for jewelers. Under the program they issue a certificate guaranteeing that they will buy back the diamond from the consumer on a dollar for dollar basis; it's a guaranteed buy-back plan.

The plan hasn't caught hold, primarily because they charge the jewelers more for diamonds sold under it. But I think it is ironic that in America they decry investment in diamonds, while in Europe they have their own investment organization! The pricing policy of DeBeers is directed at maintaining stability, even if it comes through creating confusion.

DeBeers appears to be sending out false signals in the hope of discouraging speculation in diamonds. The less speculation, the less chance there is for a sudden price surge and, ultimately, a price drop.

This effort to maintain stability can be seen in a variety of sources. I recall Harry Winston, the great diamond dealer, being interviewed on television back in 1975. The country had just come out of one of the most severe recessions since the Second World War. The questioner asked Winston what DeBeers' pricing policy had been during this period. Winston replied that they had raised prices 20 percent five times.

I can recall the interviewer reacting with disbelief. Would DeBeers actually be bold enough to raise prices during a period when all investment markets including diamonds were supposedly soft?

Winston answered that what DeBeers had done was to slightly curtail the supply of diamonds it was introducing into the market and at the same time increase the quality. This increased the profit margin for the merchants and helped them weather the stormy period

Calming the Great Speculation of 1977–78

There is an interesting corollary to this story and it happened in 1977 and 1978. It was then that everyone seemed to be discovering "hard" investments (as opposed to paper ones). People were buying real estate and gold and, for the first time, many were looking at diamonds. Individuals who might have speculated in gold were now thinking of speculating in diamonds. Large corporations with money to invest saw diamonds as an opportunity to make big profits. There were petrodollars pouring into diamonds. The potential for a market explosion in price was enormous.

Remember that in 1977–78 financing was readily available and fairly inexpensive. In Israel, for example, the financial community lends money on diamonds at interest rates subsidized by the government. During this period it was possible to get financing for 80 percent of diamond purchases. Just imagine what this can do to a market. If you have a thousand dollars to invest, but there is no financing, you can only buy a thousand dollars worth of diamonds. But with 80 percent financing you can parlay that original thousand dollars into a five-thousand-dollar investment (your $1000 plus $4000 in borrowed money). The key to it all is the anticipation that diamond prices will go higher. Back in 1977 speculators poured into the market.

At the time the popular belief was that the only place to be in diamonds was in the one-carat market. One-carat diamonds had gone up and up in value and everyone anticipated they would continue to soar.

Everyone, of course, except the DeBeers organization. They viewed the trend in the market as destructive of stability. They saw all these people moving into diamonds for the short haul as creating a potential catastrophe. DeBeers realized that these speculators would be in only for that short ride up the price ladder. Once it peaked (as it would have to do when the last speculator had put in his or her last dollar and prices started down) they would all bail out. This would cause decline in prices.

DeBeers saw that this would hurt the jewelry trade, since it would scare consumers away. It would also be potentially bad for investors, because it would turn diamonds into the same kind of roller-coaster-ride that had afflicted the gold market. So DeBeers acted. Starting in August 1977, DeBeers announced no price increase for one-carat stones, the diamonds that had been the big movers. In addition, it released sufficient quantities to meet the demand.

Now imagine if you will the board room of a major corporation. They've put a lot of money into one-carat diamonds, anticipating large profits. But there is no profit for the month of August 1977. An employee is charting their diamond investment on a huge wall graph. For August the graph looks flat. Everyone waits for the next month.

No price increase and no profit in September. Some of the directors are asking questions. Why are they into an investment that isn't making money? The management says not to worry. Diamonds move sporadically. The profit will be there. But again there is no increase and no profit in October. No profit in November. No profit in December.

Back in the board room of the pension fund the directors are now asking nasty questions. More than an entire quarter has gone by with no profits from their diamond investment. They could have made more money by sticking their investment in the bank at 5%.

No profits in January 1978, nor February, nor March. Two quarters without profit? Let's get out. That's a ridiculous investment. The corporation begins selling.

The one-carat market did not move for fourteen months! During that time DeBeers shook out the speculative interest in that market. (Fortunately, since then, pension funds and petro-dollar investors have seen the longterm benefits of diamonds and have quietly started to come back in. Only now, they're not in for the quick buck, they're in for the longterm, solid-asset investment. They're buying for ten and twenty years. They are also buying diamonds for their own "God forbid" accounts.)

Knocking Down Credit Speculation

Of course the one-carat market was not the only one affected by speculation during 1977–78. The Israeli banks, through their lending policies, had encouraged enormous speculation in diamonds during this period. But in addition to holding down the price of one-carat stones, DeBeers had held down prices across the board. It had increased supplies and not prices.

The Israeli banks were suddenly worried. They were lending money on the assumption that diamonds were going to increase in value, but they were not increasing. The banks started pulling back. They began to think "What if diamonds start to fall back?" The banks were responsible to their depositors so they cut back. Instead of lending 80 percent of the value of the diamonds, they lent 75 percent, then 66 percent. With less financing there was less opportunity to speculate. The DeBeers policy had cut down on the credit available to diamond speculators.

But DeBeers was not satisfied that it had fully removed speculators from the market. It was afraid that, even after nearly a year of effort, when prices rose the speculators would be right back in. So in March of 1978, DeBeers shook the diamond world. They invited 250 brokers to London and told them that, as of that moment, they were going to impose a 30 percent *surcharge* on all diamond sales. It was an across the board surcharge on all "rough" (uncut diamonds direct from the mines). What's more, they indicated that the surcharge might be temporary—they might remove it at any time.

Immediately telegrams and phone calls began racing around the world. We got our call within three minutes after the meeting. The diamond merchants were shocked. But the bankers were aghast. Think what it meant to the bankers. Here they were lending all but about 34 percent. But now the diamonds would have a 30 percent surcharge that could be removed without warning. When it was, it would peel back the price by 30 percent. The banks' margins would be erased and they would have exposed loans.

Immediately bank financing dropped back to about 40 percent of the purchase price—half of what they had been lending just a few months earlier! The result was that speculation was crushed. DeBeers in one action affected the entire credit picture for the banks in Israel.

Of course, we have just been using Israel as an example because it has state-subsidized financing for diamonds. Diamond borrowing is common all over the world, especially in each of the countries that house the fourteen exchanges. In one swoop, DeBeers affected the credit in all the exchanges and the entire diamond market went flat overnight. Price levels simply froze. Growth ended and the market was flat for nearly a year.

Eventually, when speculation had cooled, DeBeers began raising prices and the surcharge became part of a permanent price increase in 1980. In the first quarter of 1980 there were very large price increases. A one-carat stone went up by over 50 percent in some grades of investment sizes!

Price Movements

At this point, I think it would be helpful to get some insight into exactly how price increases work their way through the market. It is one thing to say that DeBeers raised its price of rough by 20 percent, but how is that reflected in the price that the ultimate buyer pays?

When DeBeers announces a price increase in rough for all the thousands of grades of diamonds, how does a diamond dealer in Bombay respond to that information? The dealer knows that when he goes to replace his stock he will have to pay more, but how much more? A 20 percent across-the-board price increase cannot really be understood without evaluating each type of diamond. There may be fewer investment-grade sizes, which could mean investment-grade diamonds will actually go up 40 percent. And there could be a large quantity of commercial grades, which means that jewelry-grade diamonds will only go up 10 percent. It's going to take a long time before the actual price increase is broken down for each grade and size of diamond.

All the merchant in Bombay knows is that he had better raise his prices for all his merchandise, and *fast*. Eventually the trade press will break down the grades so that everyone will know that, in certain categories (or *bands*) prices are up this much and in other bands they are up that much. But everybody is caught short with their inventory at first and all they know is that they must charge more.

Imagine that for one month, two months, or longer there has been no price increase in diamonds. And then in one month the price goes up 40 percent. You've suddenly made a 40 percent profit! I don't think anyone can compare this phenomenon, which happens regularly in diamonds, with any other market in the world.

This happened in the first quarter of 1980. The rise was instantaneous, as merchants across the board raised their prices anticipating having to pay more when they restocked. But over time the true rise per grade filtered down through the market as world inventory was in fact replaced with the higher priced goods. The increases came about in the first part of the year, but they didn't filter down to all levels of merchandise until late summer. At first prices moved up dramatically. Then they moved up slower and slower as brokers refined their information and discovered what they would actually have to pay.

Why Soft Markets Occur

We are prime-source buyers. In early 1980, when prices began to rise in anticipation of a DeBeers rough price increase, we warned our clients to be careful not to pay too much. In some grades there would be a tendency to charge too high a price in anticipation of what the new rough prices would be.

But many people ran out there and bought. Some got burned. When the precise effect of that increase filtered down to the market, it turned out that a few grades had been increased for too much—and so they came back down. Those people who had bought at the peak of excitement and then sold six months later could indeed have seen a price decrease in certain grades of diamonds. But did an overall price decrease take place? The answer is no. Those who lost did not hold long enough and got caught in the normal settling of the market. The fact remains: Rough diamond prices set by DeBeers have not declined even once since 1934. And between July 1979 and December 1980 the value of the most commonly sold investment-grade diamonds appreciated in a range from 47 to 69 percent.

When people speak of the diamond market as having taken

big drops—say 10 or 15 percent in periods such as late 1980—they are generally speaking of a few grades of diamonds that were pushed unrealistically high in price by the excitement over a DeBeers rough price increase.

There's another reason for the diamond market to go soft on occasion. In 1980 we saw an enormous increase in interest rates in the United States. This increase meant that brokers who bought diamonds on financing suddenly found it very expensive to hold their inventory. So they sold as quickly as possible to avoid the high interest rates. In order to do this they may have offered lower prices. For those who were expert in the field, who knew what to look for and how to grade diamonds, here and there it was possible to pick up a bargain stone. Again this gives the appearance of reduction in diamond price, while the reality is that DeBeers has not lowered the price of rough.

(This interest-rate phenomenon, it should be noted, normally only affects merchants. Those who own diamonds for their jewelry value as well as those who buy for investment rarely sell during such periods. They know that if they hold on for just a while longer, they stand to make significant profits.)

Usually merchants only lower their prices on diamonds for which they may have paid too much at the beginning. After all, why should they charge less when it is going to cost them more to replace the merchandise they have? The annoyance of high interest rates has to be balanced against the higher cost of new inventory.

It should begin to be clear why anyone who buys diamonds should hold them for a minimum of three years.

Minimum Holding Period

The diamond market does not move in cycles in the sense that stocks or gold do—it isn't a roller coaster. But it isn't straight up on an ever-increasing line either. It moves up, plateaus for a while, then moves up again. In order to show a profit, any buyer must purchase and then wait for a price movement upward. As I just said, months may go by when there is no price increase at all. The price just stays there for months and months, perhaps a year or even longer. But then in one month it jumps. A person buying diamonds must hold onto his precious jewels long enough to take advantage of the way the market moves and get the benefit of a price movement.

Of course if you buy just before a price increase you could show a whopping profit in less than a month. If you buy *very* timely, you could show an increase in just a few days. On the other hand, it could take as long as two or three years.

I suspect that when diamond dealers tell customers to wait at least two years, some potential buyers think that by the end of two years the dealer plans to be long gone. I hope it is now clear that they are really saying if you buy diamonds you have to understand the market and how DeBeers operates its pricing. (As an aside, never buy anything from someone you suspect will not be around in two or three years! If you are seriously worried that the person selling you any investment is going to skip after you are in, stay out.)

The Federal Reserve Bank of Diamonds

The DeBeers pricing policy has, in effect, placed them in the position of being the federal reserve banker of the diamond world. They issue the diamonds worldwide and are responsible for them as a benevolent custodian. They regard their position of trust seriously and try to use prudence and intelligence, so that generation after generation will be secure in their diamond purchases. Whether it is a small engagement ring, a lavish necklace, or a diamond investment kept in a vault—whatever it is, DeBeers with its worldwide power and pricing is there to protect it.

One diamond advertisement that I liked very much commented "Take my investments to lunch." It showed a very pretty model seated at a table. She was covered with diamonds. The ad was a bit chauvinistic since there were no men in the scene, but it got the point across that jewelry is an investment too.

I believe that DeBeers could legitimately sell all the diamonds it produces as quickly as they come out of the ground. I think that buyers will continue to exceed the number of sellers. And that is the problem that DeBeers faces in the future. I have spoken of the might of the company and its resources, but the one resource it cannot control in terms of increase are diamonds themselves.

It is my understanding that in order to keep the price stable DeBeers is spending billions of dollars developing new diamond mines across the world. It is hoped that by 1990 diamond production will be back up to the roughly 60 million carats a year of 1960. Imagine trying to get supply back to where it was over twenty years ago! And think what demand has done in the interim. There could come a day when pension funds and petro-dollars and individuals move into diamonds in such a way that they totally eat up the supply. At that point DeBeers' benevolent control of the market would finally be threatened. The giant might not be able to stabilize prices and they could soar. Of course, for present investors that is hardly a dread possibility. A big price increase would delight them.

I believe that diamonds are truly the mutual funds of the twenty-first century. Diamonds are going to behave much like mutual funds once did. In part this is because of DeBeers' dampening effects, and in part it is simply because demand is so much greater than supply.

DeBeers is an organization with influence everywhere. But everywhere it touches—from the worker harvesting the stones to the mining companies to the rough buyers to the cutters to the dealers to those who buy jewelry and to those who invest— it gives benefits. True, it is a giant. But I don't see how we can fault it just for being big. It's a *benevolent* giant. And that, it seems to me, is what really counts.

CHAPTER FOUR

The Truth About Diamond Markup

I have sometimes heard investors new to the diamond market talk glibly about the markup on these precious stones. Occasionally they will mention to one another that the stones are marked up 30 percent or 100 percent or 1000 percent or, it appears, whatever figure happens to come to their minds. When I point out that the after-tax profit margin of my company (which is the largest investment diamond importer and marketer in the world) is about 1½ percent, they are left speechless. They usually suspect that I'm not telling the truth, but truth it is.

I think the difficulty in understanding diamond markup comes from the concept that these delicate gems occur free in nature. After all, man does not make gem-quality diamonds. (Synthetic diamonds produced thus far have only been of such size and quality as to be suited for industrial purposes. Simulated diamonds such as the YAG or the Cubic Z do not compare.) The erroneous idea is that, since diamonds occur naturally in the ground, we should not have to pay so much for them. A one-carat, near-perfect stone can cost $20,000 or more. Yet someone just found it lying in soil. The thought is that nothing could justify the high price. Middle men must be making a fortune—or so goes the reasoning.

I won't deny that there is a lot of money to be made in diamonds. I have made a great deal myself. But I do submit that the horrendous markups that many people imagine are misconceptions.

The True Cost Of Diamonds

No other mineral extraction process requires the removal of so much ore for so little payoff as diamonds. Ten to thirty *million* parts of ore to one part recovered mineral is the ratio. That is unheard of in any other industry. And all this recovery, including the payment of workers, the creation and operation of machinery, and management, costs money. It has been estimated that the minimum capital investment to open a new diamond mine today is $500 million. That is half a billion for just opening the mine. It does not include the millions needed to find the site, nor the additional millions required to continue operation. Nor does it include the costs that go into "manufacturing" a diamond.

Most people probably think of a diamond only as a glistening gem set in a ring of gold. If that is how you visualize a diamond, then you might be disappointed to see this most precious of stones when it comes out of the ground. A diamond in the rough looks like a pebble or small rock, not much different from its neighbors.

It is usually translucent and is immediately identifiable by the way it refracts light, but it is a far cry from the cut and polished gem. Between the rough diamond and the cut-and-polished is a long and expensive journey. To understand diamond pricing and markup requires an appreciation of that journey.

The rough stone, once removed from the ground (whether in South Africa, Russia, Australia, or elsewhere), in 80 percent of cases is owned by DeBeers. It is sent to the Central Selling Organization in London. There the diamonds are sorted by size and grade. Row after row of experts sit at windows facing true northern light (in the northern hemisphere) and check and classify each diamond.

Sights

Once the diamonds are sorted, they are then sold to brokers at sights. A *sight* is the name given by DeBeers to the process of selling roughs to the world's diamond merchants. There are ten to thirteen sights a year, almost all held at 2 Charterhouse Street in London.

Throughout the world there are tens of thousands of diamond merchants working in every aspect of the trade. However, only the most prestigious brokers are invited to the sights. They are hardly public auctions. You cannot simply decide you want to attend, you must be invited. At each sight there are no more than 220 to 270 brokers present.

There is also very little dickering. The DeBeers executives present a "box" of diamonds to each buyer and that buyer is told the price. If he wants to look into the box at the diamonds, he may, but very few buyers do. Usually they simply pay without question. After all, where else are they going to get diamonds?

Some brokers request specific weights or grades, but I understand that such requests are rarely granted. In most cases the buyers simply have to take what they get. The price for these boxes varies, but the minimum is probably in the $300,000 to $500,000 range. Remember, that's the amount paid per sight per buyer, and when there are a minimum of ten sights per year and about 250 buyers, it adds up to an enormous amount of money.

How does DeBeers arrive at the price for its boxes? Obviously, DeBeers charges enough for the diamonds to cover the costs of mining and marketing. But the pricing is far more important than that, for by both the quality of diamonds released and the price charged DeBeers controls the world price for diamonds. The pricing, therefore, is a matter of policy as well as economics. I'm sure that on occasion DeBeers makes huge profits; I'm equally sure that on certain occasions, in order to maintain a stable world price, DeBeers actually sells at a loss. But in general the pricing reflects the costs of production plus a profit. If their profit structure is anything like ours, it is probably a fairly low percentage.

The sight buyer can pretty much do what he wants with his diamonds. Most buyers sort them, taking out the diamonds they want for themselves, and broker the rest. If a buyer wanted to, he could immediately sell the entire box for perhaps a 10 percent profit. What he would not want to do is to refuse the box or take it back. If a buyer refused a box there would be no questions asked of him. If he returned a box, he would immediately be given a full refund without question. However, he might not be asked to the next sight. Or for the next three sights he might have poorer quality material.

Once the diamonds have been purchased by brokers, they must be cut and polished. This is an expensive and lengthy process. Usually, it is not handled by one merchant. Frequently diamonds are bought and sold as many as ten times before they reach final market.

The reason for this is that there are so many different grades and weights of diamonds. Some brokers deal only in certain categories of diamonds, others prefer other categories. The trading that goes back and forth is the sorting out of the diamonds so that ultimately the right *merchant* gets the right material.

Diamond Markets

There are fourteen major diamond exchanges throughout the world; they are located in Antwerp, Tel Aviv, New York, London, Amsterdam and elsewhere. Each of these locations is governed by the World Federation of Diamond Bourses, which polices its members' integrity very strictly.

The largest market by far is Belgium, with more than half of the cut-and-polished diamond trade going through this single location. Another large market for cutting and polishing stones is Israel. There the diamond market is the country's largest single industry. In Israel the main market is in small stones and commercial goods for the jewelry trade. The stones tend to be of lesser quality and there tends to be more a production-line attitude than an artisan feeling. This is not to say that there aren't diamond artists in Israel, only that they operate mostly on a quantity basis.

I have been through the production rooms in the biggest Israeli diamond factories. I've seen hundreds and hundreds of saws running simultaneously and thousands of people at work. It is here that a major cost of diamonds occurs. To understand, it's necessary to follow the process of transforming a rough stone to a cut-and-polished gem.

From the sights in London, the Israeli diamond merchants received their rough. Some of it is not suitable for use in the Israeli plants, so it is brokered to other parts of the world. Similarly, other merchants broker part of their material to the Israelis. Ultimately the right type of stones end up in the Israeli market.

Figure 4–1

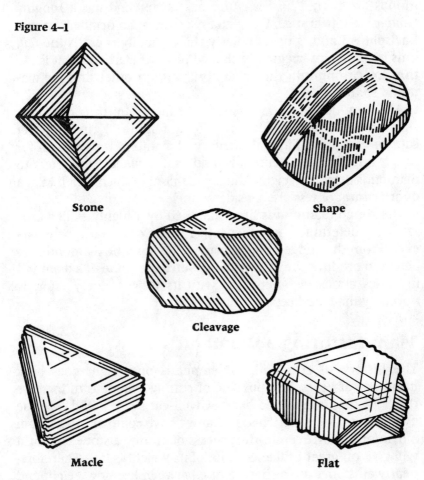

Stone

Shape

Cleavage

Macle

Flat

Grading Rough Diamonds

The rough stones are generally classified into five categories (see Figure 4–1). There is the *stone*, which is a perfectly formed octahedron. Next there is the *shape*. A shape is an octahedron that for one reason or another was formed in an irregular pattern. Like the stone it is unbroken, but it does not have the perfect octahedron appearance. Next there is a *cleavage*. This is a stone that has been broken. The cleavage was probably damaged on its trip upward from the fiery pits below the earth's surface where diamonds are born. A *macle* is the next shape and has a roughly triangular appearance. It is actually a part of an octahedron that has split off and is usually fairly thick. Finally there is the *flat*. This is simply an irregularly shaped piece of diamond that is too thin for cutting into the usual "brilliant" or other finished diamond shape.

All diamonds that are one carat or larger are thus classified. Diamonds that are smaller are usually found only in the lesser categories. One additional category of diamond is used both for rough and finished diamonds, and that is *melee*. This refers to diamonds of small weight. Usually diamonds which weigh in at a quarter carat or less are considered melee.

The rough diamond is first examined by a highly skilled artisan who determines whether it is a shape or a macle or whatever. From this judgement he can decide how the diamond is to be cut to produce the largest stone. Since the value of a diamond increases almost geometrically with its weight, every effort is normally made to keep weight.

Manufacturing a Diamond

The history of cuts with an emphasis on weight goes back hundreds of years. The purpose of cutting a stone is to increase the light that is reflected back. A well-cut stone will dazzle the eye with its brilliance. This is what we have come to expect from a diamond. However, in the process of cutting a stone so that it will give off great brilliance, a lot of its weight is lost. Therefore, nearly all stones are a compromise between keeping weight and attaining brilliance. The job of the artisan who first examines the stone is to judge what will be the best way to cut it for both weight and brilliance.

Once the artisan has determined how to handle the diamond, the next step is the actual cutting. *Cutting* is a general term which in reality simply means the manufacturing of a diamond. There are numerous steps in the manufacturing process. Usually the first is either *cleaving* or *sawing* the diamond.

CLEAVING

Cleaving is an age-old process that has been handed down from generation to generation by families who have specialized in the diamond business. It is that part of cutting which most people have seen at one point or another. In fact, I can recall a commercial in which a diamond "cutter" sat in the back seat of a car and, to prove how smooth the car rode, "cut" a diamond. What he actually did was cleave it.

The process of cleaving involves splitting a diamond by hitting it. Cleaving can only be done, however, along the *grain* of a diamond. Most people speak of grain in terms of wood, but diamonds have grain as well. The grain is along the face of the crystal. If the perfect shape of a diamond is an octahedron, then it has eight faces. Any of these can be reduced by cleaving (see Figure 4-2).

The process of cleaving is fascinating. Since cleaving is an art, every cleaver has his own tools and his own special way of handling the process. In general, however, all cleavers use a box into which the diamond is affixed. Next the cleaver takes a small piece of diamond, usually a broken chip which has a sharp edge and, using solder or some other cement, affixes it to a stick. Now the cleaver is ready to work.

He has already carefully examined the diamond, determined its grain, and with a pen marked exactly where he wishes to reduce the diamond. He now takes the diamond chip and begins rubbing it very hard on the line he has drawn. Both diamonds must be firmly affixed to withstand this process. After a time the chip will make a slight abrasion in the other diamond. This is technically known as a *kerf*.

The cleaver next inserts a specially shaped wedge into the kerf and then carefully taps it with a rod. If he has accurately located the grain, properly made the kerf, cleverly located the wedge, and applied just the right force to the rod, the diamond will instantly split exactly as he has hoped. On the other hand, if

51

Figure 4–2

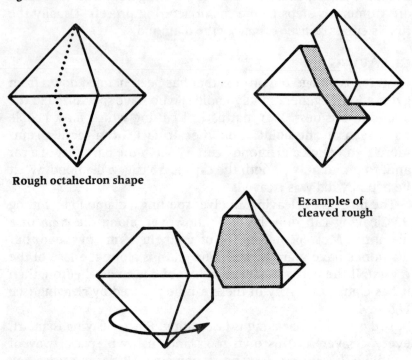

Rough octahedron shape

Examples of
cleaved rough

there has been an error anywhere along the way, the diamond may shatter.

Cleaving, since it is far more an art form than a science, is therefore usually reserved for the lesser quality stones, particularly in Israel (although some of the world's largest stones were initially reduced in this fashion). In Israel stones which in the rough are only worth a couple of hundred dollars are reduced by cleaving. They are small diamonds, heavily flawed, and usually reserved for the jewelry trade. If one shatters, no one weeps for it. They go on to the next. It is a quantity production area.

SAWING

For larger stones, or those of better quality, sawing is often the preferred procedure. The last time I was in Israel I watched the sawing of a 60-carat diamond. It had been on the saw for over four weeks! The circular saw blade is very thin and of a special type of bronze. It is about four inches in diameter and made so that it will not curl or twist. It can cut to within a thousandth of an inch of accuracy. Diamond dust prepared in a solution of olive oil which has been allowed to sit in the sun for several days (called *bort*) is then applied to the wheel. It is the action of the diamond dust on the wheel that makes the cut. Because the diamond is so hard, it takes a great deal of time to make even the smallest cuts by sawing. No pressure is applied. The diamond, positioned above the blade, is sawed by its own weight.

You might think that a diamond could be sawed in any direction like a piece of wood, but that is not the case. Though it can be cleaved in many directions, it must be sawed against the face.

The process of sawing or cleaving usually reduces a diamond to the rough shape of the finished gem.

BRUTING

The next process is *bruting*, where the diamond is actually rounded off so that it begins to reveal its final shape, though it is still smooth. Bruting is incredibly hard work and I can recall my surprise the first time I heard it—it makes an enormous amount of noise!

In bruting, the diamond is cemented onto a *dop*, a stick used for holding the gem. Then the dop is placed into a lathe. A second diamond is fastened to the end of another dop, which is fixed firmly in the end of a tool that looks much like a police officer's baton and is about two-and-a-half feet long. When the lathe is turned on, it spins at high speed while the bruter forcefully applies the second diamond (the cutting tool) to the first. By this method the diamond is *bruted* or *rounded*.

In bruting, as well as in cleaving and sawing, the diamond is always observed carefully to be sure loss is minimal and also to check for flaws. The stone will be cleaved or sawed in such a way as to cut away flaws. The placement on the lathe for bruting is similarly calculated to eliminate flaws.

Each time the bruter leans his tool into the diamond to be cut, there is an enormous *brrrr* sound, no doubt accounting for the name of the process. He examines the diamond repeatedly under his eyepiece or *curl* (magnifier), then applies the tool again. In this way, over a period of time, the diamond comes to look like a child's top. It is the shape seen in jewelry stores, but without the facets.

POLISHING

The final step in creating a finished diamond is the *grinding and polishing*. This is done by a highly skilled workman on a tool called a *scaife*. The scaife looks much like a potter's wheel. It is made of extremely hard steel and usually has a number of work areas on the surface. A ring circling the center of the wheel is the roughest area, and is used for the trial-and-error work that leads up to the final cutting. The center of the wheel is the medium surface and is the one used for the actual faceting. The outermost ring is the polishing area.

The diamond is mounted in another dop, then placed in the front of a special holder that can be held against the rotation of the scaife. The cutter examines the diamond through his curl, determines where the facet should be, and applies the diamond to the wheel for a few seconds. He then takes the diamond off the wheel, executes an agile pivot of the tool so the diamond is brought up to his eye, carefully examines to see that he has cut correctly, and repeats the procedure. This process of cutting, then examining, then cutting may be repeated more than a *thousand* times for a single diamond!

As noted earlier, a diamond may not be cut in all directions. Basically it can be cut across the grain. The specialists who do this are called *cross cutters*. They normally put on the first eighteen facets. These form the *table* or the top of the diamond (which we see when looking directly at it), the *culet* (the very tiny bottom of the back of the diamond), four *corners* and four *bezels* on the top and four corners and four *pavilions* on the bottom. (Bezels are the top facets, pavilions are the bottom facets.) After the cross-cutter has finished, the diamond may be returned to the bruter for a process called *rondisting*, in which the stone is now made perfectly round, something that may have been impossible until this time.

Finally, the diamond is turned over to perhaps the most skilled craftsman, the *brillianteerer*, who puts the final forty facets on the stone. (Today's modern brilliant diamond, has exactly fifty-eight facets.) The brillianteerer polishes the stone and tries to eliminate remaining flaws.

ROBOT MANUFACTURING

The process just described is the traditional approach to manufacturing diamonds. Today robot machines have been invented to do this. They save an enormous amount of labor cost, but nothing can compete with the human eye for judging the correctness of the diamond cut. Therefore the robot machines are generally used only for the melee (smaller) diamonds and those of low quality.

A Unique Creation

The material on which these skilled craftsmen work is extraordinarily tiny. A full carat is only 200 milligrams, or 20 percent of a gram. By the bathroom-scale method of measurement, this makes it about 1/150 of an ounce. Most stones, of course, are much smaller. Just the thought of creating fifty-eight facets on something so tiny is mind-boggling. But what is perhaps most mind-boggling of all, yet something that investors must know, is that in this process of manufacturing each diamond is made unique!

Because there are flaws unique to each rough, no two diamonds are identical. Just as there are infinite differences in snowflakes, so too are there infinite differences among diamonds. This has been demonstrated by a machines called a laser spectograph, which creates a photographic image of a diamond being hit by laser light. No two diamonds ever produce the same image. If you were to examine these photo images, you could easily see that no two images are even close in appearance!

The Cost of Waste

During bruting and faceting, perhaps half the weight of the diamond has been lost. A diamond that started out costing $500 a carat, now costs $500 per half carat. The effective cost has been raised to $1000 per carat through waste. This does not include any of cost of the machinery or labor involved.

Once the diamond has been manufactured, it must find its way to the marketplace and eventually be sold to a buyer of jewelry, a collector or an investor. This is done in the diamond exchanges. For history and flavor, we are going to change scenes now and move from Israel to the largest diamond exchange, in Antwerp.

The Antwerp Exchange

The Antwerp Exchange is like no other place in the world. I really don't think it is possible to understand diamond pricing and markup without having some appreciation for the Antwerp Exchange.

To reach the exchange you walk down a small roadway, Peligadaam Street. It is a cobblestone road with a train depot behind the building. Eventually you get to the bourse, which is the trading building. The street is always amazingly empty during the day. Toward mid-afternoon, when the trading sessions are over, it suddenly fills with the brokers. For the most part they are Hasidic Jews. They dress in long black coats and always wear black hats. To someone totally unfamiliar with the diamond trade, it might appear that you were suddenly engulfed by people from another planet. These brokers might think *you* came from another planet, if they bothered to glance up. Usually they are totally engrossed in their work.

Jewish Tradition in Diamonds

Before I describe what happens in the bourse, I think it appropriate to dispell some misconceptions about why the Jews dominated the diamond trade both in Antwerp, Israel and elsewhere in the past. (Today a sizeable portion of the industry is not Jewish.)

It began hundreds and hundreds of years ago in Europe. Actually, it goes back as far as the Spanish Inquisition. In those earlier periods the Jews were heavily persecuted. It was not like the antisemitism we see in the world today. In our world the antisemitic feeling is, I suspect, largely political. Those who are most stridently prejudiced often hope to get some political mileage out of it. Of course, there are many others who simply are looking for some scapegoat to blame for harsh economic times.

In the Renaissance period, however, the persecution was primarily religious. The Jews did not accept the religious dogma of the times and therefore were punished. The penalties imposed on those who espoused Judaism and would not convert to Christianity were often related to property. Jews were prohibited from owning property. This made them perpetual tenants, and it also made them transient. They tended to move from one city to another hoping for better conditions.

Because they could not own land, there were not farmers. Yet they had to earn a living to survive as transients in a society that was almost entirely non-Jewish. Because they were an educated people with a long history of literacy, of keeping records, and of business dealings, they found it natural to become merchants. But because they were socially outcast they found that the only merchandise they could handle was that which the regular merchants did not touch.

One of the items they merchandised was money. The Mosaic laws generally prevented one Jew from charging another Jew interest on money. But they said little or nothing about charging a non-Jew. Similarly, strict Christian dogma of the time prohibited one Christian from charging another interest on money, but said little or nothing about charging non-Christians. Therefore strange partnerships of Christians and Jews were formed where the Jewish partner lent money to Christians and the Christian partner lent money to Jews. Out of this tradition arose the stereotyped "Shylock" character from Shakespeare's *Merchant of Venice*. Most Christians of the era were unaware that some Christians were lending money at interest to Jews. They only saw Jewish merchants collecting interest from Christians. In truth only a small percentage of Jewish merchants were in the money trade.

About this time diamonds became popular and it was only

natural for the Jewish merchants to begin dealing in them. They quickly discovered ways of manufacturing and ultimately setting diamonds so they were most fashionable. Nobles and royalty in the court would order diamonds and the Jews would create the most fashionable styles. Along the way they developed highly refined techniques for cleaving.

There was another reason that the Jews got into the diamond trade. Since they were prohibited from owning property, and gold was too heavy to carry, those who had any wealth at all carried it in diamonds. They couldn't run with a wagonload of goods or pockets full of heavy gold. But if they were fortunate enough to have some wealth, and unfortunate enough to be persecuted, they could flee to another country and start over with diamonds. The Jews, being driven from one country to another, traded diamonds amongst themselves and became very good at it. Eventually the guilds that related to diamonds were dominated by the Jews. They passed their secrets for manufacturing diamonds from father to son and for many, many years totally controlled the trade.

I have been privileged to see this tradition passed on personally. As noted in the first chapter, early in developing our diamond company I became associated with Steve Greenbaum, who is now my brother-in-law. Steve is one of the great gemologists in the world, and it comes from his family background.

Steve's grandfather is Jack Serin, whose family was in diamonds in Russia for as long as anyone could remember. Serin is a great man in the diamond business. He helped to organize the First Diamond Dealers Association of Los Angeles. He has often told the story of how he lent money to famed New York diamond dealer Harry Winston when they were both young men starting their careers in the diamond industry.

Serin's family came from Russia. They lived there during the period of great persecution after the turn of this century. Pogroms were taking place. (These were organized massacres of Jews—men, women and children—often by soldiers who would race down streets killing everyone they saw.) Serin's family fled the pogroms and came to the United States. To get out of Russia they had to get emigration documents and certificates and all sorts of permissions. In addition, they were prohibited from taking any wealth with them. Eventually they were allowed to leave, but only if they left penniless.

It so happened that they had in the family a small table which they called a prayer table. It was just a place were holiday and ceremonial prayers were said. They were very observant ortho-dox Jews. Before they left Russia they spent the better part of a year methodically hollowing out the legs of that prayer table and stuffing diamonds into it.

Then, they were ready to leave. They had given up their bank accounts, furs and jewelry to the state. They were taking with them only a few pieces of clothing, a few pieces of furniture, and this crummy looking prayer table. They came to the emigration station and the Russian soldiers there made them turn over all their remaining furniture and searched them for any other valu-ables. They were trembling, afraid that their prayer table would be taken away from them and apparently the guard noticed this. But the guards assumed they wanted the table only because of its religious significance, which was very little. You can imagine that the Russian soldiers didn't even want to touch this miser-able little prayer table. They were told to take it and get out of the country.

Now imagine the celebration a month later in a New York tenement room that had been arranged for them on their arrival in the United States, when they cut open this ugly little table and took out all the diamonds that had been stuffed into it! They immediately opened a diamond business here in the U.S. Not much later the Great Depression hit and they did a furious busi-ness as people traded in diamonds to get themselves out of financial difficulties. Out of this tradition came Steve Greenbaum.

I hope this small story gives some insight into the Jewish tradition that surrounds the diamond trade. I hope it also explains why, when Hasidic Jews come out of the bourse in Antwerp and see tourists staring at them, they stare back. They are participating in a tradition that is hundreds of years old—in truth, it is the tourist who is out of place.

There is another part of this tradition that needs to be under-stood by the ultimate diamond buyer: integrity and bargaining.

Integrity

Integrity and how it is demonstrated is perhaps the most difficult thing for someone unfamiliar with the diamond trade to understand. Diamonds worth countless millions of dollars are exchanged every day in Antwerp, yet there are no documents to sign, no written contracts to look over. It is all done on the basis of trust. A diamond merchant is only as good as his eye (for *evaluating* diamonds) and his word. A word broken once may never be trusted again. Thus it is unheard of for a merchant to go back on a deal once it is made.

Steve Greenbaum is a member of the bourse in Antwerp. He is a diamond dealer who deals in hundreds of millions of dollars worth of these precious gems for our company. But if one person in one bourse anywhere in the world were to say one controversial thing about Steve, he would be denied membership in all the bourses of the world. He would be immediately banned and blackballed. Such is the power of the exchanges.

Bargaining

Every bit as strong as the tradition of integrity is the tradition of bargaining. I can remember the first time I stood outside the bourse in Antwerp. The Hasidic Jews moving in and out did not look very impressive, although I knew they could easily have a quarter-million dollars in diamonds in their pockets—maybe more!

I entered the building with the son of one of the great men of diamonds. His family too escaped from Russia, and they have dealt in the great jewels of the world. Because I was with this person, my entry was not questioned, though others were not allowed in. The bourse is a closed trading house; tourists are not permitted. Jewelers are admitted onto the main trading floor with a pass from a member, but only members of the bourse and their guests are allowed in the private trading rooms upstairs. There *patrons*, as stone owners or buyers are called, negotiate sales.

When we entered I didn't notice the guards until they were

pointed out to me. They are very discrete, so discrete that they are required to know each member's face! To know every member of the exchange they spend hours memorizing photos, an extraordinarily difficult task.

The main trading floor is enormous and there are huge windows on the north side of the building. One of the criteria for grading diamonds is color. Lack of color, called *whiteness*, is highly prized. The only way to tell the color of a diamond is to consider it in colorless light. Although today there are machines that perfectly duplicate colorless light, north light during midday is still considered the best source of colorless light. When examined against this background, any color inherent in the diamond will show.

Row upon row of tables lead out from these windows and the diamond traders sat there exchanging, buying and selling. The rough diamonds that were sold in boxes at the sights, having possibly been cut and polished in Israel, end up here on the floor of the exchange to be bartered.

Upstairs patrons from the major jewelry houses of the world were negotiating. Buyers from every country were there. Later we went to the basement, where the diamonds are kept in huge vaults. Even larger vaults contain huge amounts of money belonging to various dealers. In the diamond trade everything is cash—and trust. Only little slips of paper identify diamond ownership and cash. These people could be dealing in fish as easily as diamonds!

Perhaps nothing illustrates the bargaining better than what happened when we sat down in the bourse cafeteria. Steve, my host and I were waiting to eat lunch. But rumor had spread that Steve and this other person were in the building and before we realized it a line of brokers had queued up to show us merchandise.

My friend was shown a diamond which the broker described as "flawless." (They all knew he was looking for top-grade material.) He took out his jewelers loupe and carefully examined the stone. North light was pouring in, so he could see the diamond clearly. He put it down and looked at the broker. "Emile, did I do something to your mother? I saw her the other day and we talked. I did something that offended her or the family so that you give me this . . . this garbage! You call this 'flawless'?"

This is the beginning of trading. The merchant started at $10,000 a carat. My friend stopped at $1200 a carat and only then because, he later said, he was afraid if he got down to $800 a carat it would be the true value for the gem and he would have to buy it. Yet it was such poor quality he had no desire for it.

Emile left and the next merchant appeared and the same thing happened all over again. In virtually every case nothing was as it was represented. It was all overgraded. But that is part of the expected bargaining process. That is part of the tradition.

It soon became clear that my friend was interested in a top-quality heart-shaped diamond. Merchants throughout the building began searching for heart-shaped diamonds. We tried to dismiss the crowd that was gathering and go on about eating lunch, but they persisted. People came flying by to show their diamonds. One of them in his haste dropped an eight-carat diamond in my friend's chicken salad! He had to dig it out with his fork. And that's the way diamond bargaining is done.

It wasn't until I was leaving the building that I began to appreciate the security measures. If at any time someone did something wrong, or if someone who wasn't a member started to run, alarm buttons located at numerous spots could be hit. When that happened, in this old building that looks like a schoolhouse, heavy armorplate steel doors would slam shut and in a few seconds the entire building would be sealed. No one would be let in or out until the disturbance was explained.

At the same time, loudspeakers outside would tell people on the street to lie flat. In truth, anyone in Antwerp already knows that if there's trouble in and around the exchange, you lie flat and don't move. Guards would suddenly be everywhere, on roofs, turrets, and in the streets, all with automatic weapons. The entire block of the city could be sealed off in sixty seconds, and the entire area of the city in just a short while with the aid of Belgian soldiers.

Retribution is swift and direct, usually outside the legal system. I can recall an incident not long ago when two men, barely out of their teens, attempted to take a diamond merchant's son as hostage. (In Europe, the taking of hostages and holding them for ransom is quite popular both amongst criminals and political activists.) The men were arrested, then quite suddenly released. They simply disappeared. No trace of them was ever seen again. There was no trial. No one questioned it—it was simply understood. Anyone who tampers with the diamond merchants is not going to be seen again.

Adding Up the Manufacturing Costs

The DeBeers syndicate charges for producing diamonds from the ground. The brokers who buy at sights, then rebroker the roughs until they get to the appropriate cutters, charge for their service. The manufacturers who cut the roughs into brilliant stones charge for the waste and for their costs of production. And finally, the diamond merchants in Antwerp, who bought the stones from the cutters, try to sell the stones for a profit. Each person along the way provided a service. If he could not charge for his own costs he could not afford to stay in business.

The Marketing Cost

The final cost is that of the import and investment firm. Let's go back to Antwerp for just a moment. The reason my friend was able to negotiate reduced prices was because he was a diamond expert. He understood quality and price. But someone who does not understand these things might have paid the first outrageous price asked ($10,000 a carat). I can recall talking to a disappointed woman who, on a trip through Europe, stopped at Antwerp to buy a diamond. She said that she thought she would get a better price by going to the source. She simply asked what the price was and paid it. Later she learned she had paid five times the true value of the diamond. Needless to say she was disappointed. When you buy through a reputable import and investment firm, that firm has sent buyers to Antwerp (or some other exchange) and the buyers have used their expertise to obtain the very best price for every diamond they buy.

Our own company employs more than five hundred people

plus over 10,000 commissioned sales representatives. We occupy ten major buildings with hundreds of thousands of square feet of office space and two enormous computer systems. All of this is devoted to purchasing the finest quality diamonds at the best prices and seeing that our customers are well-informed and well-satisfied with the diamonds they purchase through us. And, as I mentioned earlier, our after-tax profit is about 1½ percent.

Retail vs. Wholesale

Yet, granting everything that has been said, you may still be puzzling "How can I invest in a field where I buy at one price and the import and investment firm I purchased from is buying at a lower price? When it comes time to sell, won't I be caught in a retail vs. wholesale price squeeze?"

The honest answer is no. Import diamond companies may charge 25 to 40 percent on the average, depending on the stone, the mix of materials, the directness with which the firm penetrates specific markets, the credit supplied, and so on. But *a reputable diamond company will buy back your diamond for at least the price you paid if you wait the minimum three-year holding period.*

At this point we need to discuss the definitions of *wholesale* and *retail* in the diamond business. I suspect that most people apply the same definitions to these terms that is applied when purchasing undershirts or shoes. But in investment diamonds, because of the costs, such a definition simply does not work. I have a definition that I believe will eventually become the regulatory standard for the industry.

True wholesale is the price that a professional diamond buyer would pay to acquire a diamond in the normal course of business and immediately be able to resell at a profit that would be considered a reasonable and fair markup in the normal conduct of his trade in the diamond industry. That is the true definition of *wholesale*.

Investors should never think that they can buy diamonds and instantly resell them at a profit. Professional diamond buyers cannot buy diamonds for any less than they do nor sell them for any less and still make a profit. If that investment buyer has the expertise and connections to go to Antwerp and buy, then perhaps he or she could get our prices. But, that person would have spent a great deal of time and money acquiring the expertise and the diamonds—probably far more in time and money than we charge in our markup!

What should an investor in diamonds expect to get in return for the buyer's markup? To put it simply, the investor is buying "a friend in Antwerp." A reputable diamond company should have an established history of success in the diamond market. In charging a markup, the reputable company should stand behind the grading of its diamonds. But that's not all. A reputable company should also keep investors well-informed on the current market value of the diamonds. In addition, the company should provide investors with current information and analyses on the diamond market. Finally, the company should have a strong record of reselling diamonds profitably for its customers—a record verified by third parties. With all these services, the normal markup on diamonds is something of a bargain.

But there is another way to look at the markup on diamonds. Diamond trade sources prove that the appreciation in diamond values has been far greater than the markup paid at the time of purchase—so much greater, in fact, that the markup seems insignificant.

I think an example from real estate will make this clear. Let's say we buy a house in Woodland Hills, California, and after three years we want to sell. We put it up for sale at $150,000 through an agent. An ad goes in the paper and potential buyers come around. We greet the buyers and say we've really enjoyed living in this house and isn't the view from the window grand?

The buyers nod as the husband examines the crack in our cement floor and the wife looks at the waterspot on the ceiling. Finally they say they like our house and will we take $135,000? We point out that the house just down the street sold for $150,000. They reply they aren't buying the house down the street and will we compromise at $137,500. Finally we agree to sell at $140,000. We've taken $10,000 less than we wanted on the price. In addition, we've hired an agent and have to pay an enormous commission. And then there are closing costs. But we never seriously complain. Why not? Because three years ago we bought that house for $85,000! We're still making a huge profit.

Yet in diamonds many people want the equivalent of a no-load mutual fund and they don't want to have to pay the services of a real-estate agent.

In diamonds, more so than ever was the case in real estate, appreciation makes the markup insignificant. I have seen the smallest investor of $500 make over 200 percent in three years. I have personally seen hundreds of millions of dollars invested in diamonds and not one person who held for at least three years ever lose money. I have seen multimillionaires—and recently pension plans, corporate profit-sharing plans and the first ERISA programs—invest in diamonds. I have seen investors make 1000 percent profit on a single stone!

The markup is an integral part of investing in diamonds. But it alone never stops anyone. Diamonds have always required that you reach a little bit deeper to buy.

Jewelry Markup

There is one final markup that we should discuss. It has to do with the jewelry trade. Not only does my company sell to investors, but also to jewelers. In many cases we can sell diamonds to jewelers that they couldn't buy as cheaply anywhere else. There are approximately 35,000 retail jewelers in the United States. Remarkably, there are approximately 27,000 wholesale operations—almost one wholesale broker for every retailer! A lot of the trading goes on just between them.

The important thing to understand is that the jewelry store has what is called in the trade a *keystone*. That is the markup that has to be charged the minute anyone walks in the door. It is the price the jeweler has to get from the customer for keeping an inventory on hand, for keeping the front doors open, for hiring sales people, and so forth. Since the jewelry trade tends to have a far lower turnover than, say, the record industry, the keystone has to be high. Each customer has to pay a relatively high proportion of the jeweler's expenses. Typically, therefore, the keystone is 100 percent or more.

When you buy a diamond set in a ring from a jeweler, you are paying at least a 100-percent markup. Of course, you usually have the privilege of selecting from a large group of diamonds displayed for your convenience in beautiful gold, platinum or silver settings.

Evaluating the Diamond Markup

The diamond markup is no mystery. It only takes common sense to see why it has to be charged. If you could go to Africa, get access to the fields, work for twenty years to find a diamond, then spend another ten years learning to cut it, you just might get it for nature's cost. But would it be worth that to you?

By comparison, the markup now charged is cheap. And when tomorrow's prices are compared to today's, it will be easy to see the true investment advantage of diamonds.

CHAPTER FIVE

How to Resell
Your Diamond

Buying a diamond is only half the process of investing—to realize a profit, we must be able to resell it. When buying a house, we know there is a market for used homes. When buying stock, we know there is a resale market. When we buy gold and silver, we are aware that there is a market for precious metals. Is there a comparable market for diamonds? Is it easy to find someone who will buy a diamond, or are we stuck with a nonliquid asset when it comes time to sell?

Comparison with Gold and Silver

It always amazes me that people are concerned about the existence of an aftermarket for diamonds. They seem to have no trouble believing that an aftermarket exists for gold and silver. Yet until very recently about the only place you could sell gold or silver was a pawn shop or a coin dealer, and often they paid less than top dollar. Only within the last year or two have there been stores that specialize in gold and silver. Even today there are very few and they tend to go in and out of business depending on the fluctuations of metal prices. Yet people readily believe a resale market for small investors exists in precious metals.

On the other hand, diamonds, which have a large and well-established marketplace, often are believed to have little or no aftermarket. If you doubt the diamond aftermarket, go to your telephone book and look up diamonds in the Yellow Pages. I don't care if you're living in New York City or in a small town in

Nevada. Listed under *Diamonds*, depending on the size of the city you're in, will be anywhere from a few to several dozen dealers, most of which will have the word *buy* written large in their ads. They want your diamond, and will pay cash on the spot for it. Now, after you've looked up *diamonds* in the yellow pages, look up *gold* and *silver.*

If you have done my little experiment, I suspect you are somewhat surprised. In most phone books there are many diamond dealers, yet there are few to no dealers in gold and silver. The number of people who want to buy diamonds is enormous; dealers are everywhere. You can get cash for a diamond in virtually any city in America, in the world. Diamonds are the ultimate banking system throughout the world.

The Yellow-Pages Diamond Buyers

The people who advertise for diamonds in the Yellow Pages are generally diamond wholesalers. They make their living by buying at wholesale and then selling at retail. (I dare you to find dealer/buyers in emeralds or rubies or sapphires. In most cases they do not exist. But diamond dealers are ubiquitous.)

They are a good place to sell. But when you sell to a Yellow-Pages dealer you must remember that bargaining is involved in the diamond business. There is always the temptation of a dealer to offer less than the diamond is worth. In this sense it is conceivable that you could be cheated when you try to resell to a wholesale dealer. However, if you bought properly, you should have a reputable certificate of grade and authenticity that states exactly what you have. This should help to eliminate the chance of someone trying to claim you have a lower grade and therefore less valuable diamond.

Additionally, I suggest that a seller going through a wholesale dealer should always get *five* bids. Take the diamond to five dealers and ask each dealer to examine the diamond and then make you an offer. After five bids, chances are you will have run across someone who is trying to cheat a little bit as well as someone who is very straightforward. The price will tell. There can be an enormous range in price offered for the same diamond. Naturally you will take the highest price. Cash is cash.

Why Buy from Me?

The question may arise "Why do these people want to buy my diamond? They can get a steady supply of diamonds from DeBeers, so why would they want to bother with mine? I'm trying to inject something into the pipeline. Doesn't that mean that I am, in effect, competing with new diamonds? Won't I have to take a penalty?"

The answer is, probably not. By the time the diamond gets to the wholesaler, it is just one step below the consumer. A diamond is still a diamond, whether the wholesaler buys it from you or DeBeers. If you have a particular cut, or grade of color or clarity, or a specific weight that he is looking for, he may even pay you a premium! You may be able to supply a diamond to the dealer that he cannot get from DeBeers through regular channels. That is why I say that when you go to resell, you chance of being offered less because it is a "used" diamond is very slight. A diamond is still the most precious stone in the world, regardless of the source, and it always commands a high price.

Finally, I think we must keep in mind that DeBeers has said (and the material offered at their sights confirms) that there is a shrinking supply of good quality material. At each sight it seems that the quality is slightly less than at the previous sight. Dealers at all levels are screaming for high-quality material and it just isn't available. Some have even accused DeBeers of hoarding the good material. DeBeers' response has been that they are not hoarding, that the high-quality material is simply no longer coming from the mines. This correlates well with the fact that most of the mines are older and, traditionally, the deeper the mine the lower the quality of stones.

To the diamond owner this means more money! If you bought a few years back, chances are you bought a higher-quality diamond than is available today. You may not have set out to do that, but you probably did simply because better material was available. Now when you sell you will reap the benefits of the drop in quality of new diamonds. You may actually find you are getting premium dollar for your precious stone when you resell.

The simple fact is that the market wants a high-quality diamond. Since it is not coming through the pipeline from DeBeers, the individual seller today is in the best position to deliver it and receive the benefit.

Can I Sell for a Profit?

I imagine some of my readers are musing "Even if I get top dollar from a wholesale dealer, does that mean I will make a profit? After all, we have been talking about selling my diamond to a wholesale dealer at a wholesale price. But when I buy I'll have to buy at retail. Where is the profit to be made in buying at retail and selling at wholesale?"

If you're looking to put one dollar in today and immediately get back two dollars tomorrow, I suggest you stay out of diamonds. This is not to say that, if your timing is right and the price makes a big jump the day after you buy, you won't be able to make a big profit. You will. But that would be unusual and lucky. If you are looking for fast overnight profits, I suggest you take your money to Las Vegas or Atlantic City. There you can double your money not just overnight, but in a few moments on the throw of the dice, the flip of a card or the spin of a wheel of fortune. Of course, the risk of losing all you invest would also be there. In fact, my understanding is that at these gambling houses the chance of losing far, far outweight the chance of winning. That, after all, is why it's called gambling.

On the other hand, if you are looking for an investment, you must be willing to wait for your investment to grow. Eventually it will give you your profit. Time is the key element.

Naturally you can't buy retail today, then resell wholesale tomorrow and make a profit. But if you're willing to wait, you will eventually be able to sell for more than you paid, and if the past is any judge of the future, you will be able to sell for incredibly more than you paid.

Making a Profit from a Cheater

Perhaps the best way to look at this is to consider a person who picks only one dealer out of the phone book when he goes to resell his diamond. Let's say this one dealer cheats him; rather than offer the true price, the dealer offers him the lowest price that is credible for the diamond. How will our investor come out?

If he had owned the stone for one year he might lose 10 or 20 percent, possibly a bit more. On the other hand, depending on the quality of the stone and the market, our investor friend could show a profit even while being cheated! The market could have gone high enough that our investor could be getting back more than he paid, even though it wasn't top dollar.

Now let's say our investor held the diamond for three years, then went to the unscrupulous dealer. How will he fare? My feeling is that after three years, even if he is cheated he will probably make a profit! He won't get top dollar, but he will get more than he paid for the diamond. Rather than make the 30 or 40 percent profit he is entitled to, he might only make 5 or 10 percent, but he wouldn't lose money.

What if our friend had held the diamond for more than three years? My feeling is that he could be cheated in the market and still make a very attractive profit. The diamond appreciation would be such that, even with a bad dealer, our investor friend will do all right.

This is one of the great inducements for diamonds. Can an investor do this with rubies and sapphires, with coins, or with gold or silver? No, he cannot. It is only with diamonds and the DeBeers syndicate controlling the stability of the market that this works.

Diamond Gains vs. an Index

Do you still have some hesitation? Perhaps it is a concern because diamonds are not a paper investment. I talked about paper investments earlier and I honestly think they have been bad for most people. Yet Americans still seem to like paper. Perhaps this is a holdover from the days when stock-market mutual funds did well.

We particularly like to be able to consult an index—a price comparison between then and now. The stock market has the Dow Jones averages. Gold has the London price fixing. Real estate advertises the median prices of houses sold. It seems every other investment has its value index. "How can I invest in diamonds," some people ask, "if I don't see that index moving up so that I can feel confident of liquidating? How can there be a true aftermarket for diamonds without an index?"

There is simply no connection between the price of diamonds and an index. The diamond market is unlike any other, and it is not an index market. Everyone wants to bring diamonds to a level at which it is possible to determine what is a uniform price for an understandable component. But, there are thousands of grades of diamonds—perhaps tens of thousands!

Diamonds are not interchangeable. When you buy a diamond, you are buying a portable work of art. Each diamond is a small Rembrandt or Picasso. It is more or less perfect depending on the stone from which it was cut and the art of the cutter. Each diamond in the world, as we've seen, is unique. So when we come down to pricing for resale, how can we have one index that would accommodate millions and millions of unique pieces? It would be like trying to have an index for snowflakes.

Let me put it a different way. At a given time, the rate of appreciation for one diamond may not be as high as for another. The one-carat market may be moving, but melee and half-carats may be sitting still. Or high grade colorless stones may be in higher demand and may be appreciating faster than other grades. Each diamond or diamond grade has its own rate of appreciation, and that rate varies depending upon a wide variety of factors including supply/demand and popularity. This is why an index of the price of diamonds is literally impossible. There never has been a true index and I doubt that there ever will be.

But this lack of paper verification of the price of diamonds should not be a deterrent to buying. The fact that we don't have an index of sales values does not mean that there aren't sales or that the price of diamonds isn't rising. It simply means that for this particular investment form, an index is not appropriate.

Diamond Investment Companies

Thus far I have only talked of liquidating diamonds through wholesale dealers—those who list their names in the Yellow

Pages. But there is another method of reselling a diamond, one which many people prefer. That is to sell the diamond back to the investment firm from which you bought it.

As I've noted, investment-grade diamonds comprise only about 1 or 2 percent of all the diamonds that are harvested each year. Since very few diamonds are harvested (only about 40 million carats, or nine *tons*), there really aren't a great many diamonds available to sell for investment purposes. This wasn't really a problem a few years ago as most of the investors were Europeans. However, with the big American market waking up to the potential for diamond buying, the entire picture has changed. Where once there was an adequate supply of investment-grade diamonds, today we are seeing a shortage.

This has had many different effects. For one, the grade of diamonds which is considered investment is being lowered. When there aren't enough of the top grades to go around, the lesser grades suddenly become popular. For another, it has made it increasingly hard for diamond investment companies to acquire top-grade material. Investment companies such as ours send buying teams around the world searching for top grade material. How much easier it would be if we could find that material right at home!

This means that a reputable diamond company has tremendous potential as an aftermarket. A reputable company will offer to liquidate the diamond you bought from it a few years earlier and give you your profit. If the company you bought from is a straight-shooter, you'll get top dollar without having to go around to five dealers for a comparative shopping list (although I encourage that, nevertheless, as a way to confirm that the company you're dealing with is reputable).

In our company for example, we will liquidate any diamond we have sold to our customers and we will be happy to get it because we can resell. As it turns out, the vast majority of our customers refuse to sell. They want to hang onto their diamonds. They are aware of the appreciation taking place and their only reason for selling is because they have a sudden need for some cash. Other than that, why sell? What would they do with the cash profits they made? Probably just stick them back into diamonds.

74

Another reason we are so happy to buy back our own diamonds is because, when we sell them originally, we give the customer a certificate of authenticity and grade from our own IDC Trade Lab. This certificate is like a pedigree and guarantees the quality of a diamond. But not all certificates are equally valued. We automatically question a diamond with less than an IDC certificate.

Few People Actually Sell Their Diamonds

In the past, most people bought diamonds for jewelry purposes. Even today, probably 80 percent of the diamonds sold in the United States and around the world are for this purpose. What this means is that most of us do not buy with an eye toward reselling. We buy because we think the diamond is precious, because it has romantic or sentimental meaning, because our parents bought diamonds, because of a thousand reasons other than investment. Most of us buy diamonds because we instinctively recognize this brilliant stone as having a special significance.

The result of this is that few people actually sell. How many of us would think of selling the diamond ring we received for our wedding? Would we want to sell a special diamond necklace given by our spouse or a very special friend? Would we think of cashing in a diamond stick pin or broach or pendant that is a family heirloom? These are the last things we would think of selling. These diamonds would be among our most prized possessions. They would be a mark of our wealth and our achievement in the world. They would signify how far we've come.

I suspect that before actually selling, many people would turn their diamond over to a pawnbroker and anticipate coming back to redeem it within a few weeks. The idea of a total and final separation of a diamond from its owner is painful. Once we have a diamond, as the famous DeBeers' commercial says, it truly "is forever."

As I've noted, this holds true for investors as well. Why should an investor sell his or her diamond unless there is an emergency and a sudden need for cash? What would the investor do with the profits from the sale? Just reinvest in diamonds.

But in spite of the fact the relatively few diamond owners

actually do sell their diamonds, in spite of the fact that diamonds are forever and investors won't easily part with them, in spite of all these things, we should not believe that an aftermarket does not exist. It is as close as the Yellow Pages or the nearest representative of your diamond investment company. The aftermarket is large and ready to buy your diamond anytime you can bear to part with it.

CHAPTER SIX

Diamond Banking

We have already seen how Peter and John, of our primitive society, gave up the barter system in favor of money as a medium of exchange. Since then, many different materials and objects have served as money. Often there have been several different *kinds* of money from which to choose.

Today that choice is one of the most important ones you will make. With the financial uncertainty that faces us, and the possibility of world-wide calamities, it is crucial to choose the best kind of money.

Diamonds as Money

Diamonds are an ancient form of money. They were part of a money system used by cavemen. They were used by individuals long before the time of Christ. Huge armies have gone to war over them. Roman legions invaded eastern lands searching for them. Napoleon financed his last war campaign with them. For hundreds of years they kept the Czars in power in Russia. Today diamonds are helping modern investors around the globe to maintain and increase their wealth. "But it's not fair to speak of diamonds as money," I have heard some people say. "Money is cash—dollar bills, yen, Deutschemarks."

No, that's not true. Money is anything that will facilitate the exchange of goods and services (as we saw in the primitive society of Chapter 2). In the history of our own country, gold and silver struck in the form of coins served as money. In ancient times carob seeds and abalone shells served as money. In the Yap

Islands in the Pacific giant round stones taller than a man serve as money. Money is not simply the ubiquitous paper of today—it is anything that can be used to make a purchase. (Credit cards in our modern world are as real a form of money as dollars and they are made of plastic. Plastic, therefore, can be money!)

Diamonds, too, are money. Diamonds can be used to make purchases. Diamonds are a medium of exchange. Diamonds represent buying power. What makes diamonds outstanding is not just that they are money—they are the *best* money!

The Best Money

Suppose we are back in 1970 and we want to buy a car. A typical car in those days cost about $5000. Let's further say we had a diamond that was then valued at $5000. Could we buy the car with the diamond? Of course we could. We might directly barter the diamond with the car dealer, if he happened to be familiar with diamonds. Or if he were not, we could sell the diamond, get the $5000 in paper money and make the purchase. Either way, the diamond represented *purchasing power* for us.

Now let's suppose we kept that car for ten years, until 1981, then decided to trade it in on another car. Could we get a new car for our older one? Hardly. We'd be lucky to get $50 for a ten-year-old car. Could we get a new car for the $5000 we paid in 1970? Not likely. Today a typical car costs closer to $10,000.

Could we get a car for the diamond?

Let's say we somehow had the very same diamond back. It was no bigger, it hadn't been recut. Would we be able to buy a typical car with it today?

You bet we would! That diamond would have appreciated in value until it was worth the price of a car today. The diamond would retain its purchasing power while the car and the dollars lost theirs. For all practical purposes, therefore, the diamond represents better money. (If the truth be known, the same diamond that bought a Chevy back in 1970 could buy a Cadillac today. The diamond not only kept pace with the inflation seen in paper money, it beat it by far. The diamond actually increased its purchasing power relative to dollars.)

78

It is this aspect of diamonds, the use of diamonds as super-money, that has engrossed so many Americans over the last few years. From taxi drivers to plumbers to politicians to oil sheiks, diamonds have become extraordinarily attractive.

DIAMOND MONEY VS. GOLD MONEY

Recently gold has been much in the news, as Congress has been asked once again to put the United States back on a gold standard. The gold standard is touted as a panacea for our economic ills. But will gold really work?

What does the government want? It wants stability in its currency. It wants to defeat inflation. Some people think it can get this by ending paper money and creating gold money.

It is a noble goal, but to me a hopeless one. Just consider the price of gold over the past few years. It has been up and down and all over the place. In January 1980 if you went into a store with a one-ounce gold coin, you could buy roughly $800 worth of goods! Six months later it was back to about $650 and six months after that to nearly $400. What kind of stability is that? What kind of anti-inflation money is that? What kind of investment is gold? Gold as anti-inflation money is ridiculous. And silver makes no more sense.

If paper money submits to inflation, if gold and silver are unstable and therefore unsuitable as money, what alternative is left? I submit that the only alternative a rational person will find is diamonds.

VALUE HISTORY OF DIAMOND MONEY

The conservative financial publication *Trusts and Estates*, which serves the managers of pension funds and trust accounts, has taken a hard look at diamonds. It traced the price performance of diamonds from 1905 to 1975. That's a long period of time—seventy years. It found that, during that period of time, investment diamonds had increased in value at a rate of 12 percent a year.

That rate of appreciation is really phenomenal. It is better by far than gold, than silver, even than the stock market or real estate. It is better than anything else in the world!

This survey ended in 1975. Since that time the appreciation rate of diamonds has accelerated. The rate has been much greater than the former 12 percent a year.

SAFETY OF DIAMOND MONEY

Diamonds as money are more than just inflation positive—they offer *safety*. We have discussed the fact that diamonds are rare, perhaps the rarest object when the ratio of ore mined to mineral recovered is considered. In addition, they are manufactured. Each diamond is unique, created by an artisan. The result of this is that the value of diamonds can never be diluted. Paper money can be inflated simply by chopping down more trees and printing more dollars. Gold can be inflated just by melting it and adding copper or another base metal to the mixture. But what can be done to diamonds? Diamonds remain intact from their creation until the end of time.

Additionally, because of the reduced supplies of diamonds (down to 37 million carats by 1979 from nearly 60 million carats back in 1960) as well as increased demand, diamond value and marketability is virtually guaranteed. It is impossible to think of a time when diamonds will not be considered objects of value. They have a history of value going back over four thousand years. I fully believe their value will continue for four thousand years into the future. Four millenia from now, our paper money will not exist. Gold and silver could be so plentiful as to make them useable in children's toys. But diamonds will still be able to buy a car, or a space shuttle, or whatever other vehicle is used for transportation.

And, finally, to guarantee the safety of diamonds we have the magnificent DeBeers syndicate. Its policies of stability insure that diamond value will not have bumpy cycles, but will be steady.

There is no other commodity on earth to compare with the safety offered by diamonds. But safety is not the only side benefit. There are still others.

OTHER BENEFITS OF DIAMOND MONEY

Privacy is an important side benefit of diamonds. Diamonds are small. You could take all your wealth—including bank accounts, real estate, stocks, cars, furniture, everything—and reduce it to just a handful of diamonds. Then you could put that handful of diamonds into your pocket and no one would know it was there. The government won't regulate it. The diamonds become a very private form of money.

Portability is another side benefit. As we saw with the rulers of South Viet Nam, just try getting out fast with 10,000 ounces of gold. Just try getting through an airport security X-ray machine with a suitcase full of silver. Just try stuffing your pockets full of currency and not be noticed.

But a fistful of diamonds can be transported in the hollowed out leg of an old prayer table or in a shirt pocket. Diamonds won't slow you down with weight or with bulkiness. They are the most compact form of money known to man.

Flexibility is also an attribute of diamonds. It is not necessary to buy one large diamond. In fact, I advise against it. We can buy from many different diamond groupings. We can mix our investment and then, if we need to cash it in, sell only that part of the diamond portfolio which has moved upward, saving the rest for later needs.

The Danger of Not Recognizing Diamond Money

Our society today has a financial illness and, as members of the society, we suffer from the effects of that illness ourselves. Yet it is an insidious illness whose sources are difficult to locate. The illness is very much like a cancer, eating away at the financial health of our society.

We earn wealth, but then lose it to inflation or poor investments. It is eaten up by all the frustrating ways we try to save, such as putting paper money into stocks, bonds, savings accounts, gold, silver, and on and on. We know the financial disease is eating away our wealth, but we don't know how to cure ourselves. We are losing money, but we don't know way.

Now enter the world of diamonds. Suddenly we have a cure for the financial cancer we have been experiencing. Imagine the excitement a cure for physical cancer would generate! If you had

81

the cure, wouldn't you want to tell everyone? That's why I'm so enthusiastic about diamonds. That's why I have converted my money into diamond money. Diamonds are the cure for financial cancer.

How to Get Diamond Money

But how does one actually convert diamond money? I have talked about buying diamonds, but how is that like money? Money is something you can put into your wallet. Do we put diamonds into our wallet? In a sense, yes. The way to obtain diamond money is through diamond banking.

Diamond Banking is Discrete

I personally learned about diamond banking in the mid-sixties. At the time I made the acquaintance of a "discrete" banker who told me how to obtain diamond money. Discrete banking is something at which the Swiss excel. It is something I wish everyone could appreciate at some time in their life. It is banking like no other kind. There is no ostentatious bank building, nor is there a row of teller windows inside. Instead, discrete banking involves dealing directly with the banker himself.

A discrete banker will be located in a building that you could very well pass by without noticing. There might be a doorman who would politely stop you and ask your business. You would mention who you wanted to see and that you had already made an appointment. The doorman would then recognize you (you were right on time, as the Swiss typically are very prompt) and you might take an elevator, escorted, to a third floor. There you would wait in a small area until someone came and took you to a cubicle where you would handle your business.

This is the way you open a Swiss bank account. It's also the way you could handle diamond banking. You see, the bank in Switzerland does not deal exclusively in currency, as do nearly all U.S. banks. It also deals in gold, silver, or whatever else the client may wish—from purchasing quantities of food to petroleum. As a significant function, these banks obtain diamonds for their clients.

It is no more unusual to go to a Swiss bank and deal in diamond money than it is to go there and deal in Swiss francs. The discrete banker realizes that for a large proportion of Europe's population diamonds are considered money.

So much for the Swiss version of discrete banking. What good does that do an American in St. Louis or Los Angeles or Boston? There are relatively few Swiss bank branches here in the United States. But there is a source.

Diamond Banking in the U.S.

Some diamond investment companies have instituted a program of diamond banking. It is possible to deal directly with these companies in *diamond money*. Diamond banking in the U.S. is almost exclusively handled in this way. Since I am most familiar with how our company handles diamond banking, I'll use it as an example.

We use diamond passbook accounts. These accounts look much like the dollar savings account you open in a bank or savings and loan association (see Figure 6–1) but they are radically different.

Each time a saver buys a diamond, a precise description of the diamond is recorded in the passbook, along with the amount of the transaction. The diamond goes into the saver's safety deposit box in his other bank and the passbook is kept with other financial documents at home. This is not at all like a typical dollar savings account. When you put money in there, you only get the passbook back. You certainly do not get the passbook *and* the money.

That, of course, is one of the beauties of diamond banking! You get to hold the actual asset in your hand! They can never close the bank on you. They can never change the rules of deposit on you. Your guarantee is not that they will chop down more trees and give you more paper when you ask for it. Your guarantee is that you hold the diamond in your hands.

Figure 6–1

But, if the buyer holds the diamonds, why have a passbook? The passbook records the value of the diamond asset. It gives a running account of how much your diamond is worth when converted into dollar money. For example, let's say that when you begin your diamond assets are worth $1000. Six months later, their value suddenly jumps to $1300. We update our passbooks continually. In this case, the next entry would post the additional $300. The diamonds, of course, haven't changed. The saver still has them. What has changed is their value relative to dollar currency. That change is shown in the passbook (see Figure 6–2). The diamond passbook shows the saver just how much his or her diamonds are worth at any given time. It is a record of diamond wealth.

We have in our computer banks the same records that appear in the passbooks of our savers. To sell their diamonds and convert to cash, all the savers need do is make a phone call. The passbook can be immediately updated and a liquidation (cash conversion) figure quoted. A consignment liquidation, subject to receipt of the diamonds, can actually be handled over the phone!

Figure 6–2

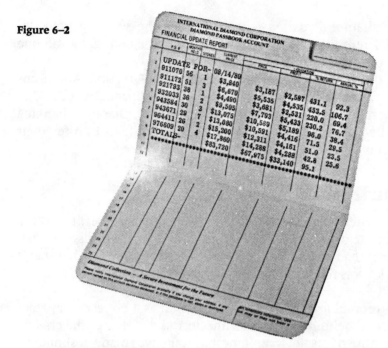

This is a little different in form from transferring money from one dollar account to another in a bank, but there are enormous differences in substance. In a bank savings account the interest received, even in the highest paying T-bill accounts, is *inflation negative* after taxes. In a diamond passbook account profits have been inflation positive, even after taxes! (Remember: Diamond profits, like real estate or stocks, when held for more than one year are eligible for reduced capital-gains tax treatment.)

Diamond Passbook vs. Bank Passbook

It is important to differentiate between traditional bank savings accounts and a diamond account. The two quite literally have nothing in common with one another. Your bank account operates differently and serves you differently. A diamond account is a specific method of transferring wealth into an asset in which you are the controlling factor. No outside company or group of individuals controls your wealth or can influence the value of your merchandise. The world diamond market—and only the

85

world diamond market—can influence the value of your deposit. There may be no FDICs in diamond banking, but no one can close the bank down on you.

At the present time, approximately 127 million Americans store over $1.6 trillion in commercial banks throughout the U.S. Many millions are looking for a better way. Diamond banking may be that better way for those who wish to transfer their capital wealth into the twenty-first century.

Security of Diamond Banking

Most experts agree that diamond grading is in reality only a statement of opinion. If that is the case, isn't it possible that, when we go to resell, the investment company can say that a mistake was made? What would happen to our diamond money then?

No reputable company would do that. All honest companies will stand behind their lab certificate and not change the grading at the time of resale. If an honest mistake was made, it should be the responsibility of the investment company to suffer any loss. A reputable company will offer passbook savers either the full original purchase price or the current liquidation price— whichever is *higher.*

Diamond banking is a concept that is used to help us see diamonds as real money. It is a concept where you not only get an updated inventory of your asset, but the asset itself. You never have to worry about the bank doing something with your money that could get you into trouble. You hold on to your money yourself.

Some people have grasped the concept of diamond banking so well that they are using the passbook plans as annuities. They buy diamonds until retirement, then they sell a thousand dollars a month or ten thousand dollars or whatever and live off the diamond wealth they have acquired.

Perhaps the most vital part of the whole concept comes from the fact that when we make a deposit in a diamond passbook we are participating in the largest bank in the world! It has branches in every country in the world and in every major city. There's *always* a place where a diamond can be sold.

Diamond banking is not new, it's old. What is new is the paper money that we have become accustomed to over the last century. Diamond banking in one form or another was in existence even before the world invented paper.

Paper investments are children of inflation, and they are doomed forever to be children. They will never reach adolescence or maturity. The paper money, the stock, the bond, whatever is the child—inflation is the adult. Inflation always stunts the growth of the paper child.

Diamond banking on the other hand has a full growth cycle. Diamonds are children when we buy them. As they remain in our possession, an asset recorded in our diamond bankbook, they truly grow. Their purchasing power increases. Ultimately, they mature and we have real wealth. The diamonds appreciate in value; they grow up and we receive the benefits. For the person who puts them to good use through diamond banking, they are also the way to grow rich.

CHAPTER SEVEN

The Treasure
of the Ages

W e have talked about diamonds as being inflation positive. We know that they are the best insurance against disaster and can provide a "God forbid" account that is unparalleled for both portability and enduring value. We have seen the advantages of a diamond banking system. These are sound, rational reasons for investing in diamonds. But we must not overlook the reason that most people buy diamonds.

Diamonds have their greatest appeal because of their beauty, their romantic history and their mystery. In short, there is a *mystique* about diamonds that is unmatched by any other investment known to humankind. In this chapter we will explore some of the unusual properties that make diamonds so alluring, discuss the great diamonds in history, and take a look at the story of diamond mining.

The history of diamonds is shrouded in antiquity. In all probability diamonds were highly prized long before man could write of his past. I have a friend, Ammon Bentor, who is an antiquities expert in Israel. He has spent decades excavating and uncovering the ancient secrets. He told me a story not long ago that I shall never forget. It has to do with the observation of the traditional Jewish holiday of Passover.

Diamonds in Ancient Israel

In ancient Israel, while the Temple still stood in Jerusalem, there were priests whose function it was to care for the Temple and administer to the people. During the Passover celebration a priest would don a breastplate covered with jewels and go into the sacred Temple. Only there and only on that day could he utter the name of God. It is now believed that the central stone on that breastplate was an enormous diamond. Superstition among the people held that, if God had heard, the stone would shine more brightly when the priest came out than when he went in. Therefore the people watched the stone for a sign that God was pleased. This caused an uproar among the rabbis, who argued that the watching of the stone constituted the worship of a graven image, which was forbidden under Mosaic law.

Romans in India

History tells us that Alexander the Great moved ever eastward in an attempt to expand the empire that later became Greece. However, few historians note that one important part of his move was the search for diamonds. In fact, his trek into India was apparently motivated almost entirely by the search for diamonds. Later, Roman legions followed Alexander's route with the same goal. Apparently the Indian war lords of the time created an army of sixty thousand workers, not to fight the Romans, but to bury the diamond fields! They reasoned correctly that if the Romans found no diamonds they would leave. The Indians did their job so well that even after months of searching the Roman troops failed to find the diamonds.

Diamonds in Ancient Writings

Plato, the Greek philosopher, wrote that he believed diamonds to be living beings descended from the stars. This conception of diamonds as living things persisted for nearly 2000 years!

Pliny the Elder, in Ancient Rome, had read of Alexander's search for diamonds in India, and in his own writings reported that diamonds had been discovered in a special valley. Pliny wrote that diamonds were resistant to blows (not true) and that an anvil could be split in two by the force of a diamond (true). He also noted that a diamond is associated with ram's blood, perhaps drawing on Plato's early writings about diamonds as living stones. The "Valley of Diamonds" was reported centuries later by Marco Polo, and may have been the area of India where Roman legions searched.

Strange Beliefs About Diamonds

During the Middle Ages diamonds, like gold, were believed to have healing power. While gold was believed to prevent illness, a diamond was thought to sense poison. Placed in a vial containing deadly poison, the diamond was said to grow dark. This belief may have come in part from the hardness of the stone. It was thought that poison would be unable to penetrate the surface of the diamond and would therefore lie on that surface, darkening it.

Another reason for this belief may have been that, while water beads up and rolls off a diamond, grease will stick to it. (This extraordinary property has been used in diamond mining. Raw ore containing diamonds passes in a stream of water over heavy grease. The waste is washed away, but the diamonds stick to the grease.) It is easy to imagine how an unscientific mind could have associated water with purity and grease with poison.

For awhile it became common practice for members of royalty to ingest diamond dust in the hope that it would neutralize any poisons administered by their enemies. Much as we might sprinkle salt, these rulers would sprinkle diamond dust on their food. Some reported that it had a distinct taste, sometimes sweet, sometimes salty. This custom had unfortunate results for several rulers including Frederick II, Emperor of the Holy Roman Empire, who reportedly died in 1250 A.D. after being fed a large dose of powdered diamond. I know of no studies on the results of eating diamond dust, but I can hardly believe it would be good for the digestive system.

Diamonds have been said to have other extraordinary attributes. For example, if taken to bed and warmed by the body, the diamond would heal skin sores. If placed on the head of a lunatic or one believed to be possessed of the devil, the diamond had the power to draw out the evil forces. If worn on a shield in battle, the diamond would break an enemy's sword (which probably came from the knowledge that diamonds were extraordinarily hard).

To add to the mystery of diamonds, it was well-known even in ancient times that a small percentage of diamonds flouresce or give off a different color when exposed to ultraviolet light, and some even retain sunlight and then give off a glow in the dark.

The Properties of Diamonds

Perhaps the biggest misconception about diamonds has to do with the brilliant stone's hardness. The MOHs scale, which measures all objects in the world in terms of hardness, gives diamonds a 10—the hardest object known to man. A diamond will cut all other objects in this world; nothing can cut a diamond save another diamond.

However, hardness is not the same as brittleness. As noted earlier, the diamond is by nature a crystal. A sharp blow to its crystalline structure will cause a diamond to break and, if it is done indiscriminately, the diamond may shatter into a thousand pieces. Most people assume that because a diamond is hard it cannot be broken. This assumption goes back centuries.

In the early days of mining—in South Africa, India, Brazil and elsewhere—miners were often cheated by this misbelief. Those who had laboriously dug in the soil and finally discovered a diamond took it to a broker. The brokers would often look at the stone and say it didn't look like a diamond to them, but one sure way of telling was to hit it with a hammer. If it didn't break, it surely was a diamond. The miner would agree, and the broker would place the diamond on a rock and hit it. Naturally it shattered. The miner would leave, dejected, and after he was gone the broker would carefully pick up the pieces of the broken stone and sell them.

The diamond's strength, however, is not imagined. The diamond is extraordinarily precise structurally. What this means, besides hardness, is that the diamond is not in the least malleable; it won't give or budge when pressure is exerted against it. This can be seen by the old experiment of placing a diamond in a steel vice (not recommended for readers) and gradually applying pressure—the diamond will resist. Ultimately, if sufficient pressure is applied, the diamond will actually cut through the surfaces of the steel vice.

And finally there is the matter of using a diamond to cut another stone or glass. While it is true that a diamond, being the hardest substance known to man, will cut any other substance, the fact that a diamond is subject to shattering precludes any of us from testing our diamonds on the nearest pane of glass. Once a diamond has been faceted to reveal its natural brilliance, the edges of the facets are vulnerable. Slashing a diamond across a pane of glass may indeed score the glass, but it could also chip the diamond. Considering the price difference between a pane of glass and a diamond, it would be far cheaper to take the glass to a window shop and have it cut professionally.

Diamond Jewelry

The extraordinary physical properties of diamonds, coupled with their presumed mystical powers, was undoubtedly responsible for their first being worn in jewelry. However, for thousands of years only royalty or the priesthood wore them.

Perhaps the most famous of the early jewelry pieces that contained diamonds is the crown of St. Stephen, a national treasure of Hungary. It contains numerous uncut diamonds. The crown was created in the eleventh century and has been a symbol of Hungarian self-determination ever since. During World War II, to keep it from falling into the hands of the Nazis, it was sent to the United States. Here it was kept under lock and key, first at Fort Knox and then at the West Point bullion depository.

After the war, the Hungarian government sought to have the jeweled crown returned but, because of the Russian influence in that country, the United States demurred. It was, however, finally sent back during President Carter's tenure in office, after we were given assurance that it would remain in Hungary and not be removed to Russia. The crown is easily recognizable because the cross on the top has been knocked crooked. Tradition keeps it from being straightened, and it has become known as "the crown with the tilted cross."

Over the centuries it became popular in the royal courts to wear diamonds inset into gold, and diamond jewelry was born. Agnes Sorel, mistress of King Charles VII of France, wore it to the French court as a symbol of an intrigue she was having with another man, who happened to be a diamond merchant. The association of the diamond with love has persisted to this day.

Marie Antoinette raided the French treasury and sold a number of huge diamonds, including the luckless Hope, to raise money. Despite the Queen's earlier actions, Napoleon was able to have diamonds in his crown jewels. Ultimately Napoleon used the jewels to finance his last wars of empire.

Russia's Czar Nicholas was counting on diamonds to pay for a return to power when it became clear that he would be deposed. The wedding crown of Alexandra and Nicholas, the last of the Romanovs, contained over 1000 diamonds! Alas it was not to be, and today the crown resides in the Smithsonian Institution, a tax-shelter gift from a wealthy private investor.

Today diamond jewelry is worn in every country of the world. Increasingly, brides in the United States and elsewhere prefer diamond wedding bands over all other types.

Although only a fraction of all diamonds discovered in the world are gems suitable for jewelry or investment, these are the stones society values most. It has been estimated that, since the time man first learned of diamonds, less than 200 tons of diamonds have been discovered, and perhaps only twenty tons were of true gem quality. This is over the *entire history* of mankind. By comparison, gold, the most desired metal, is produced at the rate of some 1400 tons *per year*. It is incredible to think that something so rare, so difficult to find as diamonds, is possessed by nearly every family in America! This combination of rarity and desirability makes diamonds the true treasure of the ages.

Great Diamonds of History

THE KOH-I-NOOR
No doubt the most recognized diamond in history is the legendary Koh-i-noor. Its name means "mountain of light," and it was

93

probably discovered in India nearly 4000 years ago! It has appeared again and again through history as conquering nations have stolen it from the royal treasures of the vanquished. It has its place in Indian history, as well as that of Persia and even England. It was first cut in the sixteenth century into an enormous rose shape of 186 carats.

The stone eventually ended up in possession of the East India company, which presented it to Queen Victoria. The Queen reportedly could not understand the fuss over the diamond because it was so dull. In order that it give off more brilliance she had it recut in 1862, and the weight of the stone was reduced to below 110 carats. It did then shine brilliantly, and Queen Victoria treasured it until her death. It is today among the crown jewels of England.

THE CULLINAN

Without question the largest stone ever discovered was the famed Cullinan. It was found in 1905 and weighed in at an unbelieveable 3106 carats! Roughly one hundred major stones were cut from the rough Cullinan for a total of about 1100 carats. Nearly 2000 carats were lost in the cutting process!

THE HOPE

The Hope diamond may be the great diamond most familiar to Americans. It has long been associated with tragedy. The origin of the stone is something of a mystery. Some believe it to be part of the Tavernier, a diamond of deep blue color brought from India to Europe in the seventeenth century by a French diamond merchant. Originally cut to give it maximum weight, the great diamond was recut for brilliance by order of Louis XIV and reduced to 67 carats. Its tragic legend began when the diamond was associated with the French Revolution and the downfall of the royal family. After the Revolution, the diamond disappeared.

The stone reappeared in the early nineteenth century. However at this point its weight was 44.5 carats. It was bought by Henry Hope, a diamond collector, and took on his name. Hope's son inherited the stone, then lost his fortune—including the diamond. Again it disappeared, only to resurface a few years later in Turkey as the property of a sultan who also died tragically.

In the early twentieth century it was sold to Mrs. Edward McClean of Washington and the tragedy deepened. Mrs. McClean's only child was killed in an accident, her family split up, she was ruined financially, and eventually she committed suicide. Though not all these events took place during the period she owned the stone, Mrs. McClean's bad luck has been associated with the gem.

The Hope was bought in 1949 by famed diamond dealer Harry Winston of New York. It brought him ill fortune as well, but he could never sell the stone, since no buyer could be found who did not fear the legend. Winston eventually donated the Hope to the Smithsonian Institute where it now resides. I find the Hope particularly interesting because I trace the decline of the United States both politically and economically to 1958, the year Harry Winston gave this country his present.

THE EXCELSIOR

The second largest stone ever found was the Excelsior. Again Africa was the source and the stone weighed in at about 1000 carats in the rough. For ten years it proved to be a white elephant for the syndicate that owned it because no one was willing to take on the risk of buying and cutting it. Eventually it was cut, with the largest stone being 70 carats.

THE ORLOFF

The Orloff diamond was also discovered in India and was perhaps 320 carats in weight. It, like so many other gem diamonds, came from the famed Kollur mines near Golconda.

The Orloff is originally believed to have been cut and set in an idol in a Hindu temple in South India. It was then known as "the eye of the idol." Supposedly a French soldier disguised himself as a Hindu, gained access to the temple, and pried the stone out with his knife.

He quickly sold the stone and it made its way via numerous sales to Amsterdam where it was cut into the shape of a half egg. There, in 1775, Prince Gregory Orloff saw it. According to legend he bought it as a gift for Catherine the Great of Russia, hoping it would encourage her to marry him. She accepted the diamond, then turned him away. Today most experts believe the stone is still part of the Russian royal jewels that are held in the vaults of the Soviet Union.

THE STAR OF THE SOUTH

The Star of the South has long been one of the premier jewels of the world, probably because of the enormous size it obtained in cut form. It was found by a woman laborer working in a mine in Brazil and, according to legend, she was given a pension for life for the discovery. (This is one legend that may very well be true. In order to encourage workers to hand over great finds, mine owners have typically rewarded them handsomely.) It was eventually cut into a diamond of about 130 carats, roughly half its weight in the rough.

THE REGENT (PITT)

The last diamond I will mention is the Regent, or Pitt. This is unquestionably the most beautiful of the great stones. It was discovered by a slave in India about 1700, again near Golconda. Rather than turn the diamond over to his owners, the slave decided he would attempt to steal it. To get it out of the mines, the slave purposely slashed his arm so that he bled furiously. He then wrapped the wound in cloth and concealed the diamond in the wrappings. Because of his wound he was excused from working, and he escaped. Eventually making his way to the coast, he attempted to barter the stone for a trip to another land where he would be free. The captain of the ship took the stone and killed the slave.

It was eventually sold to Thomas Pitt (for whose grandson Pittsburgh, Pennsylvania, was named) who had it cut into a brilliant shape of about 140 carats in England. To cut the stone, the diamond workers used a metal wire which had been coated with diamond dust. It took twenty-two months to cut the stone and when finished it was one of the finest and most brilliant large stones ever manufactured.

Eventually the stone was sold to the Regent of Louis XV, who was then a boy. The stone was renamed the Regent.

During the French Revolution the diamond was stolen, only to emerge later as part of the treasure of the revolutionary government. It was eventually sold to pay for maintaining the French armies. It was temporarily moved to Berlin, but eventually bought back by the French.

During the Second World War, the armies of Hitler attempted to confiscate the Regent, but it remained hidden. After the war it was presented to the Louvre in Paris.

How Diamonds are Created

The old expression "Gold is where you find it" implies that the yellow metal is located indiscriminately on the earth's surface. While this may or may not be true for gold, it certainly is not true for diamonds. Diamonds are located only in a very few special sites.

Diamonds are born in the caldron of the earth, perhaps as deep as one hundred miles below the surface. There, incredible heat and pressure act upon certain chemicals to produce these remarkable crystals. Exactly how the process occurs and what minerals go into diamonds is still something of a mystery.

For example, molten lava is usually about 2,200 degrees Fahrenheit. Yet at that temperature diamonds will actually burn! The inference is that they are born at lower than molten rock temperatures. Traditionally it has been assumed that diamonds came from carbon. However, synthetic diamonds have been made from graphite. Scientists in Russia have even had luck in producing synthetic diamonds from methane or marsh gas.

Adding to the mystery is the general belief that, when formed, diamonds are perfectly crystalline in shape (a three-dimensional octagon). Although they may have been large or small crystals, it was in this shape that they came into being. Yet when they are found diamonds are sometimes whole, sometimes broken and chipped, sometimes simply dust. The inference here is that they were damaged on the journey to the surface from deep inside the earth.

The age of diamonds is also a mystery. Since they have almost always been found in areas of great stability, it is assumed that they were formed long after the formation of the earth, perhaps as long as half a billion years afterward. On the other hand, the theory that they came about in fairly recent geological times, say less than 50 million years ago, does not bear too close examination, since some of the earth taken from diamond mines has been shown to be nearly two billion years old. Perhaps the most intriguing theory is that they were created over an enormous span of time and spewed forth from the earth in a continuous process. It may be that even today deep below the crust of this planet new diamonds are being born that will not see the light of day for a hundred million years!

Kimberlite—Where Diamonds are Found

Diamonds are always found in two types of material. The first is in a substance called kimberlite, which is apparently blue in its natural state. This accounts for the "blue" earth that diamond miners traditionally sought. The second is in alluvial planes—in terraces near the ocean's edge and occasionally in potholes in riverbeds. Most scientists assume that these alluvial diamonds originated in kimberlite and were then washed away.

Kimberlite when exposed to air nearly always oxidizes, and when it does, it turns yellow. Miners in the early days soon learned that looking for "yellow" earth was more productive than searching for the blue variety, particularly since the blue earth near the surface was usually oxidized to yellow.

Kimberlite is composed of a wide variety of minerals, most interestingly including nickel. Since nickel is frequently the catalyst used in producing synthetic diamonds, many scientists believe that kimberlite itself is the primordial soup from which diamonds were born.

Kimberlite occurs in *pipes*. Pipes are enormous fissures going thousands of feet down into the earth. They are shaped roughly like a carrot. They are wide on top and narrow on the bottom. At the very bottom they dwindle off into tiny veins reaching to unknown depths. It is possible that kimberlite is formed deep in the earth's crust or just below it and then forced under pressure to the surface. This could account for the many "broken" diamonds found in the material; they were damaged on the journey.

Kimberlite pipes can be very small at the top or very large. Some of the largest are many miles across. Originally, it is believed, they were higher than the surrounding plain and may have looked like a small volcano protruding from the surface. Over time, however, erosion has swept away much of this uppermost layer and some pipes actually appear as slight depressions in the surrounding plain.

This is most unfortunate, since hundreds of years of mining have proven that the quality (in terms of size and grade) of gemstones recovered from the pipes *decreases* with depth. The best stones are at the very top. By the time a pipe is dug to the 500-foot level the quality may be cut by 30 percent or more. In some mines it is down by over 70 percent!

For the investor this has vital ramifications. Most of the mines in operation today are relatively old. The uppermost layers have already been carved away and mined. This means that only the lesser quality ore remains and each year poorer and poorer quality diamonds will be produced. This makes existing high-quality stones more valuable.

It is interesting to speculate on the quality of the diamond-bearing ore that originally protruded far above the surface of these pipes. If the quality of diamonds decreases with depth, it is not unreasonable to assume that it increases with height. The very top of these ancient pipes may have been a veritable treasure chest of these exciting stones.

The Diamond Coast

Of course, the diamonds at the top were not always destroyed. Being the hardest substance known to man, they usually survived most forms of erosion and were carried downstream where they were later deposited in silt. The best known location of such alluvial diamonds is along the diamond coast of South-west Africa. There the Orange River flows through the kimber-lite formations and diamonds have been found both in the river and in terraces at the ocean's edge for miles up the coast.

Diamonds Around the World

Diamond mining operations occur in about a dozen countries including Tanzania, Botswana, Zaire, Congo, Lesotho, Angola, Rhodesia, Swaziland and South Africa on the African continent. There are also extensive diamond mining operations in Russia in at least six different locations. In the past, extensive diamond mining operations have been conducted in India and in Brazil. It is thought that in the future new mines may be opened in China and Australia, although early reports indicate that these are mar-ginal diggings where the quality of stone may be far lower than from the old holes. It may very well be that we have already mined the very best diamonds that we are ever going to get from the earth.

Diamonds in Brazil

About the turn of the eighteenth century, diamonds were dis-covered in Brazil. Almost all locations were of the alluvial type. To mine them, men worked in rivers. They would have to dig down to the diamond-bearing or *diamondiferous* soil and then haul it to specially constructed washing huts. In these washing huts an overseer would carefully watch as natives washed through the gravel ore searching for the elusive precious stones. Throughout the history of diamond mining, the overseer or guard at the washing site has always been present, a reminder of the great value of that which is sought. A laborer might acquire a lifetime's wages if he could steal only one precious diamond.

South Africa's Diamond Mines

About the time the mines in Brazil were playing out after only about thirty years of serious mining, diamonds were discovered in Africa. The first African diamond was found in the land of the Hottentots about 1860. Since diamonds were until then unknown in Africa, most brokers and miners refused to believe the news of the great discovery. However, in 1867 the Eureka diamond (of about 11 carats when cut) was authenticated and a diamond rush began to the Dark Continent. It gained momentum when a year later the Star of South Africa, a diamond of incredible weight (83.5 carats in the rough), was discovered by a South African near the Orange River.

At first the prospecting was sporadic. Typically, Africans would scour the countryside using fingers and toes searching for the precious crystals. Soon, however, serious pick-and-shovel miners arrived and laid a series of claims near the Vaal River. About this time the Boers and the British were squaring off in South Africa and the territorial claims of both included the diamond fields. For a time there was even talk of an independent "Digger's Republic"!

The DeBeers Mine

The first of the South Africa kimberlite pipe mines was not discovered until the 1870s, and then mining began on a much larger scale. About this time two brothers whose family name was DeBeer leased out a portion of their farm to a miner on the condition that he pay them a percentage of all that he found. When he found a great deal, miners from all over stampeded to the area. Dry claims, or mining that was done without water, covered all of the DeBeers land and they were helpless to prevent it. In the end, they sold out in disgust for a sum reported to be about $15,000. Most guesses are that the farm eventually yielded diamonds worth about two billion dollars!

The Beginning of the DeBeers Syndicate

Cecil Rhodes is generally considered to be the father of diamond mining in South Africa. He arrived late on the scene—in about 1871. He was unlucky at first in digging claims, and at one point had to resort to selling ice cream to support himself! This taught him that almost as important as the mining were the supplies the miners needed to work. He went into a partnership with others and bought pumps that could be used to clear out flooded mines. These he then leased to miners, often making more money than the miners themselves were getting from the diggings. With the profits from his pump company, he bought mining claims and, partly because he was in poor health, hired others to operate them. Within ten years he was the second largest mine owner on the continent.

The largest mine owner was a man named Barney Barnato. Barnato arrived in the mine fields a few years after Rhodes and, as the story goes, attempted to sell cigars to the miners. His cigars were reportedly so bad that they "poisoned" several miners and he was nearly hanged for selling them.

In 1880 Barnato and his brothers took a huge chance. Using money they saved, they went against the conventional wisdom of the time, which said that the hard blue ground found near the center of the mining area was barren of diamonds. They bought up mining shares for next to nothing from miners who thought they had worthless claims. When the truth was discovered it turned out that Barnato owned the heart of the famed Kimberly mine.

Rhodes by now was the principle owner of the DeBeers mine and he proposed a merger with Barnato and the owners of other mines. Barnato at first refused, but then Rhodes pulled off a remarkable trick that convinced Barnato to join. At a meeting he called for diamond buyers, Rhodes set out over 200,000 carats of the precious stones in 150 different piles, each pile containing a different grade. He negotiated the sale of the diamonds, then suggested that the merchants withhold the diamonds from the market for several months. This would prevent an oversupply in the marketplace and an accompanying depression of diamond prices. (Typically, prices rose when production was limited from the mines, and then plummeted when the mines released what they had dug.)

The merchants refused. Then Rhodes tipped over the table which contained all the diamonds. They all fell into a trough which he had previously arranged and landed at the bottom in a special wooden box. At first Barnato and others present didn't grasp the significance of what Rhodes had done. Then it dawned on them. It would take at least several months to resort the diamonds. That would effectively keep them off the market during that time. And during that period, the price would remain constant.

The trick showed Barnato that the mine owners working together could directly influence diamond prices for the better. Barnato capitulated and DeBeers Consolidated Mines Limited was formed with Rhodes and Barnato the principle owners. By the turn of the century Rhodes had wrestled control of all the mines away from Barnato and others and was himself the diamond king of Africa. He died in 1902.

The company Rhodes formed continued to be influential in diamond mining. However, new finds in other areas of Africa coupled with its own problems in raising capital to develop mines, plagued it through the first two decades of this century.

Oppenheimer and Anglo-American

Another company was born about this time. Immediately after the First World War an Englishman, Sir Ernest Oppenheimer, organized the Anglo-American Corporation. His initial purpose apparently was to gain control of some of the gold fields of South Africa and then market the gold in England and America. Oppenheimer, however, soon became interested in diamonds. He bought several mines and grouped them under a company he called Consolidated Diamond Mines of South West Africa. It was a subsidiary of Anglo-American.

By the end of the 1920s, Oppenheimer had effectively gained control of much of the DeBeers company that Rhodes had formed. But then the Great Depression hit. All investments plummeted and the demand for diamonds was seriously affected. Mine owners had for years been familiar with the boom-and-bust cycles of the market. But this seemed to be a bust cycle to end all others. It was in the mid-1930s that Oppenheimer got *all* the producers of diamonds together with the government of South Africa and formed the Diamond Producers Association.

Diamond Producers Association

Today the Diamond Producers Association is the lead diamond corporation within the Anglo-American Corporation. The Diamond Producers Association has what amounts to three subsidiaries: The *DeBeers Corporation*, which runs most of the mines in South Africa; the *Diamond Corporation*, which handles mining outside of South Africa; and the *South African government itself*. (By this definition, the corporation is bigger than the government!)

A fourth corporation, and perhaps the most important for those in the diamond trade itself, is the *Central Selling Organization*. The Central Selling Organization, which has come to be known as the CSO, is the company that offers diamonds for sale to brokers throughout the world. The entire organization, for convenience sake, is referred to as the DeBeers syndicate.

How Diamonds are Mined

Over the years diamond mining has progressed from the pick and shovel to sophisticated techniques using heavy machinery. Today the mines are operated both in open-pit fashion above ground and through deep holes underground. After some preliminary separation of the diamond-bearing material from the taking, an electrostatic separator separates the diamonds further, and then the ore is passed over a grease belt. Diamonds, since they adhere to grease, stick to the belt. (Since they cannot be wetted they are unaffected by the slow flow of water. Other minerals, however, are pushed aside by the water stream.)

In more sophisticated mines, X-rays are used to make diamonds flouresce so that they can be electronically identified and removed from the ore. Ultraviolet separation on the same principle is also used, as are other forms of optical separation. In most mines, however, each piece of the finally processed ore is carefully scanned by eye, the ultimate tool, to pull out the diamonds.

The lesson to be learned from this processing of ore is that very few diamonds are to be found in relation to the amount of ore. It has been estimated that it takes something like 30 million parts of ore to yield one part diamond!

Today, mining for diamonds in water is also a more complex arrangement. On the Diamond Coast of Africa, huge dikes of sand are constructed with heavy machinery and then the over-surface of sand is removed. This diamondiferous ore is carefully dug out and sent to a plant for processing.

Diamonds, from mystique to mining, are truly a world unto themselves. I know of no other mineral, no other manufactured product, that comes close to having the diversity, yet the uniqueness, of diamonds.

CHAPTER EIGHT

Diamond Certificates and Grading

People usually think of diamond grading as a science and it is, in fact, quite scientific, using prescribed scales and measuring devices. But ultimately it is an art. The grade of a diamond depends in great measure on the eye of the grader. In grading, having a "good eye" is everything.

This puts diamond purchasers in the uncomfortable position of buying something the value of which they probably cannot judge for themselves. Since grade determines price, they have to rely on expert opinion. In the case of a reputable dealer, this is no problem at all. On the other hand, in the case of a seller who is either unscrupulous or ignorant, it could be a serious problem. How do you know for sure the true grade of the diamond you are thinking of buying?

The need for accurate grading of diamonds—for grading that investors, collectors and consumers can rely on—has led to the creation of laboratories that specialize in this field. These labs issue certificates that state the grade of a diamond and are used to help determine price.

Grading Labs

Let's say that Jerry has decided that he wants to buy a diamond. He is convinced of the investment potential and ready to make the move. How does he go about it?

Jerry is not a diamond expert. He doesn't have an "eye" for diamonds. He can't grade them. If he looked at a diamond through a loupe, he probably wouldn't know what to look for. A court would never recognize him as an expert witness in the field, no matter how many diamonds he owned. So how does Jerry know he will get what he is paying for?

In America we're paper conscious. We want some sort of guarantee written out on paper. As long as we can see it spelled out in writing, we feel secure. Jerry is in that situation. He wants some sort of document to prove what he's getting is the real thing.

Certificates

What Jerry is looking for is a certificate that will state the grade and quality of his diamond and give an estimated value. So his first question to the diamond seller is "Do you provide a certificate?"

Assured by the salesperson that he will get a certificate, Jerry is satisfied and may decide to buy. Most of the time this is fine, of course, but in truth Jerry has bought a certificate rather than a stone.

There are perhaps two hundred companies in the United States that offer diamonds for investment. As far as I know, every one of these firms offers certificates. Since many of them realize that lots of buyers are just as indiscriminating as Jerry, they do the same thing Jerry did: They buy certificates too. Rather than sending qualified diamond experts out in the field to buy the best stones available, they ask their buyers to locate impressive certificates. It is simpler and cheaper to buy diamonds that are already certified and ready to sell.

This is a relatively new phenomenon. Just a decade ago a diamond buyer bought from a dealer he or she trusted. When Harry Winston sold a diamond, he almost never gave a certificate with it. His name backed up the stone. Yet today, I would guess that probably 85 percent of the diamonds originally sold by Harry Winston have been certified.

The Origin of Diamond Certificates

This didn't happen by accident. Perhaps the person most responsible for certificates in the United States is Steve Greenbaum. Back in the late sixties and early seventies, Steve was competing in the diamond trade in Los Angeles—a very tough market. There were buyers and sellers from Harry Winston's organization and others with large resources at their disposal. But Steve came up with an innovative idea. He told jeweler customers that he would give them a laboratory grading certificate absolutely free.

At the time there were perhaps only three other people in the country doing this, mostly from labs in New York. No one knew about certificates. In fact, no one even bothered to grade diamonds under one carat. But Steve did. He met the competition by offering a price and a free certificate, which the buyer could give to an insurance company for appraisal purposes. He put not only a laboratory analysis on the certificate, but also an appraised value—an estimated retail replacement cost. Steve built a company that initially sold diamonds to jewelers and eventually grew to become our own IDC lab, the second largest in the world.

The True Value of Certificates

If certificates are this important, the question must arise whether they are all valid. I would guess that in many cases they are not very accurate. There are dozens and dozens of labs that certify diamonds. These labs are aware that buyers are looking for certificates, so many of them grade their diamonds upward. They don't grade for liquidation (resale), they grade to give the highest price upon original sale. And many of those diamond companies who know they are going to be selling certificates to people like Jerry, go to the labs that offer the sweetest certificate.

This reminds me of the old advertising routine about a can of sardines. The sardines are bought by the first buyer for five cents. He turns around and sells the can to a new buyer for a dime. The next buyer sells the can for a quarter, and on and on. Eventually, one of the buyers decides he's hungry and opens the can. "Ecch," he says. "These sardines taste terrible. Why anyone would pay five cents, let alone their current price, is beyond me!" To which the person selling the sardines replies, "These sardines aren't for eating. They're for selling."

Certificates can be much the same way. An unscrupulous lab may greatly overgrade. An unscrupulous dealer then buys the wrongly appraised diamond and sells it to a customer. The customer in turn sells the diamond and its certificate to someone else. Trouble comes when a potential buyer opens the can of sardines—when that buyer is himself a diamond expert or shows it to someone who does know diamonds. Then the whole scam falls apart.

In the United States at present there is no regulation of certificates by any federal agency. It can be a wide open market in which the buyer had better beware. That is, it is a wide open market *unless* the buyer obtains a certificate from one of the labs that are well-known for their high standard.

In these high-standard labs I would include our own International Diamond Corporation (IDC) trade lab in San Clemente, California, the United States Gemological Services (USGS) lab in Santa Ana, California, the Gemological Institute of America (GIA) lab in Santa Monica, California, the American Gem Lab (AGL) and the International Gemological Institute, both in New York, and the European Gemological Lab (EGL) in Europe. There are other labs that grade well, but in my opinion, these are the tops. (Note: Three of these are located in California because the pre-eminent American school for gemologists is in Santa Monica, and graduates tend to settle nearby.)

It is important to understand, however, that some labs that grade horribly have been known to rely on the good name of these reputable labs. For example, having a "GIA-trained gemologist" grade your diamond is not the same as having the GIA grade it.

At IDC we issue about 12,000 diamond certificates a month (see Figure 8–1), and we have been approached by other companies and even other labs who have said, in effect, "We'll grade to any standard you set, regardless of the true quality of the stones, if you will just give us your grading business."

Even when you get a good certificate, what is it worth? Is it a guarantee of value, or even of grade?

Figure 8-1

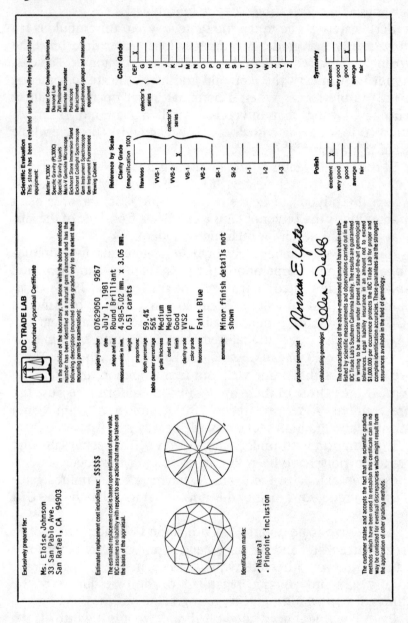

Exclusively prepared for:

Ms. Eloise Johnson
33 San Pablo Ave.
San Rafael, CA 94903

Estimated replacement cost including tax: $$$$$

The estimated replacement cost is based upon estimates of stone value. IDC assumes no liability with respect to any action that may be taken on the basis of the appraisal.

Identification marks:

- Natural
- Pinpoint inclusion

The customer states and accepts the fact that the scientific grading methods which have been used to establish this certificate can in no way be contested for eventual discrepancies which might result from the application of other grading methods.

IDC TRADE LAB
Authorized Appraisal Certificate

In the opinion of the laboratory, the stone with the below mentioned number has been identified as a natural gem diamond and has the following description (mounted stones graded only to the extent that mounting permits examination):

registry number	07629050 9267
date	July 1, 1981
shape and cut	Round Brilliant
measurements in mm.	4.98-5.02 mm. x 3.05 mm.
weight	0.51 carats
proportions:	
depth percentage	59.4%
table diameter percentage	56%
girdle thickness	Medium
culet size	Medium
finish	Good
clarity grade	VVS2
color grade	F
fluorescence	Faint Blue
comments:	Minor finish details not shown

graduate gemologist   *Norman E. Yates*

collaborating gemologist   *Allen Webb*

The characteristics of the above-mentioned diamond have been established by scientific measurements and observations carried out in the IDC Trade Lab's Southern California facility. The results are guaranteed in writing. To guarantee our present state-of-the-art gemological tolerances, legal liability insurance in an amount not to exceed $1,000,000 per occurrence protects the IDC Trade Lab for proper and complete identification accuracies. These guarantees are the strongest assurances available in the field of gemology.

Scientific Evaluation
This stone has been evaluated using the following laboratory equipment:

Mettler PL300C
Specific Gravity (PL300C)
Specific Gravity Liquids
Mark-V Gemolite Microscope
Eickhorst Stone Immersion Stand
Eickhorst Coldspit Spectroscope
Gem Instrument Spectroscope
Gem Instrument Fluorescence
Viewing Cabinet

Master Color Comparison Diamonds
Diamond Lite
ZVI Photometer
Millimeter Micrometer
Polariscope
Refractometer
Miscellaneous gauges and measuring equipment

Reference by Scale
(magnification 10X)

Clarity Grade		**Color Grade**	
flawless		DEF	X
VVS-1		G	
VVS-2	X	H	
VS-1		I	
VS-2		J	
SI-1		K	
SI-2		L	
I-1		M	
I-2		N	
I-3		O	
		P	
		Q	
		R	
		S	
		T	
		U	
		V	
		W	
		X	
		Y	
		Z	

collector's series

Polish

excellent	X
very good	
good	
average	
fair	

Symmetry

excellent	
very good	X
good	
average	
fair	

110

Perhaps the best-recognized certificate comes from the GIA. (Since they run the school, many people assume their certificate is the ultimate.) Yet there are numerous disclaimers on their certificate. Why? Because ultimately it is just a statement of their opinion. Expert opinion, but opinion nevertheless.

Most labs even have a disclaimer at the bottom or on an accompanying page that says they cannot be held responsible even for negligence! They want to be held harmless for anything that could possibly be wrong. I believe that the IDC certificate is the only one of its kind that is guaranteed *and* has an errors-and-omissions insurance policy backing us up.

Diamond Grading

In order to understand the certificates, it is really necessary to understand a little bit about the grading procedure itself. In terms of grading, the four "Cs" (carat weight, cut, clarity and color) are what determine a diamond's value. The relative weight given to one C or another, however, differs from time to time along with fads and trends in popularity. That is one reason that some diamonds suddenly shoot up in value. This happened in the late 1970s when diamond color suddenly became extremely important. Those who had the top color grades, yet had not paid an overly high premium for their originals, suddenly found their diamonds were soaring in price.

Another factor of the four Cs which should be quite apparent is that getting a properly graded stone is of critical importance when buying a diamond for any reason. An improperly graded stone, off by even one grade in color or clarity, can mean as much as a 25 percent reduction in price! The same holds true for cut, and most certainly for weight, although weight is usually far easier to determine than the other grading criteria.

Uniform Grading Language

In the United States many of the grading standards were established by the Gemological Institute of America. In addition to its trade lab and school, the GIA operates a research laboratory where it creates new tools and machines of use to gemologists. The grading standards and language established by the GIA are widely accepted in the industry.

All diamonds are graded into four major categories of carat weight, cut, clarity, and color. The quality of a diamond within each category helps to determine its ultimate value. We'll consider each separately.

Carat Weight

The weight of a diamond is measured in carats. Originally a carat related to weight of a carob seed. Today a carat is 200 milligrams or one-fifth of a gram. Carat weight at one time varied greatly from country to country, but today it is standardized.

A diamond's value depends more on weight than any other single factor. And a full one-carat diamond is not merely two times as valuable as a half-carat diamond. Twice as big does not mean a doubling of price. Rather it would be closer to a quadrupling of price! This comes about because of the increasing rarity of diamonds as they get larger. The increase in value of a diamond is a geometric progression. The larger the stone, the larger the price. That is why determining weight is so critical.

The measurement of weight is done today using an electronic scale. The scale must be balanced before each use and operates in a controlled atmosphere (that is, it must be sealed off from currents of air or any other disturbance that might affect weight).

At our labs we measure the weight of diamonds out to three decimals, then correct down to the lowest two decimals. What that means is that if a diamond weighs .999 of a carat, we would not grade it as 1.0, but as .99. The result is that the buyer always gets the benefit of any marginal weight difference.

In diamonds, one carat is said to be 100 points. This comes from the decimal expression of one as 1.00. Half a carat, therefore, is 50 points, a quarter-carat is 25 points, and so on. Generally speaking, diamonds below roughly a fifth of a carat (20 points) are considered melee and referred to only in points. Dia-

112

monds above are usually given a carat evaluation such as quarter carat or half carat.

The buyer who orders a diamond of, say three quarters carat, almost never gets exactly 75 points, however. Although we speak of cutting as "manufacturing," diamonds *are* creatures of nature and occur in random sizes. Therefore, such a buyer may have to take a 73-point stone or a 77-point stone. A half-carat buyer might get a stone of 45 to 55 points. A quarter-carat buyer might get 23 to 27 points. In the industry these variations are still considered full fractional-carat size. Of course, the buyer normally is charged only for the actual weight purchased.

Cut

Cutting diamonds goes back well into the Middle Ages. The object in cutting diamonds is to increase each stone's brilliance and the problem was that these crystals were so hard that it was a long time before anyone could discover how to make appropriate cuts.

The first cuts were accomplished by cleaving. The cutter would strike the diamond along its plane. This developed a *point cut*—basically a sharply defined octahedron. Not until centuries after the point cut was perfected did someone discover that greater brilliance could be achieved by creating a "table" on top of the diamonds (see Figure 8–2).

The *table cut* was probably the first formal diamond cut. It was considered a window into the jewel and the many ways light was reflected from it dazzled the viewer.

Figure 8–2

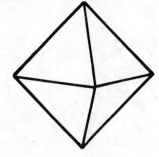
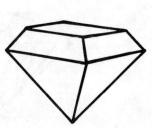

Rose Cut

About the same time the table cut was developed, a different kind of cut also came into popularity. This was called a *rose cut* because the bottom of the diamond was cut flat and then a great number of facets were cut onto the top. The crystal popped forward, seeming to open with light and thus to resemble a rose. The rose cut, however, lacks the single smooth surface of the table cut through which a great deal of light may be reflected. It eventually gave way to more modern cuts that yielded more light.

For centuries diamonds were either rose cut or table cut. Eventually the table cut became more sophisticated, with facets placed around it to enhance the brilliance. During the eighteenth century it became popular to put several facets, or pavillions, below the girdle of the diamond to further enhance its brilliance. (The *girdle* is the widest part of the diamond and generally divides the stone between top and bottom.)

Brilliant Cut

It wasn't until the present century, however, that the *brilliant cut*, which we have come to expect in a diamond, finally was discovered. The man who created it was Marcel Tolkowsky. Using mathematics, he was able to determine what he felt were the precise angles and relationships of the *crown* (the part of the stone above the girdle), to the pavillion (the part below the girdle). His work produced a diamond that shown as none ever had before (see Figure 8–3). It was an instant success and extremely popular. To this day the Tolkowsky cut is considered the

Figure 8–3

ideal diamond cut (with slight modifications in recent years, such as increasing the length of the lower facets).

The modern brilliant is the standard of diamond cuts. There is, however, an American and a European version. In America the European version is considered less valuable and in Europe the American version is lower priced.

Culet

In the brilliant cut a second table is created at the very bottom of the pavillions. This is called the *culet*, and it both reflects light and avoids a sharp bottom point that might easily be damaged.

While the modern brilliant cut is the ideal, there are numerous diamonds that, because of the way they occur in nature, are simply not suited to the round shape. The brilliant cut, therefore, has been adapted to a number of shapes other than round. These include the pear, oval, heart, and marquise.

For investors, the only cut considered investment grade is the modern brilliant, usually in the round form. Any other cut would immediately decrease the value of the gem.

Producing a modern brilliant cut produces a large amount of waste. Therefore, in order to get the most desired cut of today, the cut that will produce the highest price, the manufacturer has to give up a great deal in the weight of the diamond. What is gained in price by cut is often more than offset by loss in weight. What is a manufacturer to do?

Inevitably some manufacturers discovered that they could change the precise proportions of the Tolkowsky diamond ever so slightly and increase the weight. The resulting stone, though not having precisely correct proportions, in many cases is accept-

Figure 8–4

115

able, particularly as jewelry. Very often an expert can tell these stones by a quick examination. For example, too deep a pavillion would make the center of the stone appear to absorb light—it would be dark (see Figure 8-4).

In addition to changing the proportion for weight advantage, there are other reasons that the proportions may be changed. The original rough may simply not have lent itself to perfect proportions. Or the diamond manufacturer simply may not have cared enough, or even been able to, create a precise *make* (manufacturing according to precise dimensions). This can result in any of a great number of imperfections, including a girdle that is too thick or too thin, a diamond that is lopsided, off-center or angled one way or another.

Polish

Finally, there is the matter of polish. In the modern brilliant cut there are exactly 58 facets. But, it is not enough simply to cut the facets. They must be highly polished, and the edges where one facet joins another must be cleanly made. (In some cases a diamond may have an extra facet. This happens fairly often when a brillianteerer adds a tiny facet onto a regular facet in order to remove a flaw in the stone. If these extra facets are tiny, they are not usually considered to affect the cut negatively.)

As I mentioned, an expert can tell the quality of the cut with a simple eye examination. But, for precision the GIA has developed a proportion scope. This is an extremely handy device that can instantly show even the unskilled person whether the diamond cut is correct. The diamond to be examined is placed inside and a light is shone past it. This causes the diamond to cast a shadow on a screen. Also on the screen are projected the exact dimensions of an investment-cut diamond. By lining up the diamond in question with the investment dimensions, any variations immediately stand out.

Pricing the Cut

In grading a diamond we always give a full price to an investment cut. However, as the cut deviates from the investment proportions, a percentage of the value that is ascribed to cut is deducted. For example, a diamond that is a very good cut, but still not "investment," may have 4 percent of the value deducted. (Remember, other parts of the value are given to carat, color and clarity.) A poorly cut diamond, one that is substantially off, may find its value depreciated by 20 percent or more.

Cut, therefore, is a critical feature in determining a diamond's value. A diamond which is otherwise investment grade, could lose a great deal of its value by having a bad make.

I should point out that, on occasion, the manufacturer gives the diamond a good make but it is later damaged by the owner. This can come about when a diamond is used to cut glass or other material and an edge of a facet is chipped.

For broken diamonds or those with bad makes, remanufacturing is sometimes possible. This is exactly what it says it is. The diamond is given back to a cutter, who using a wheel, recuts and repolishes the stone. In the remanufacturing process, however, there is always a certain percentage of additional waste. Sometimes the waste is only a point or two. But other times it can be much greater. Therefore a careful judgement has to be made as to whether remanufacturing or recutting the diamond will increase its value sufficiently to overtake the loss that will occur from the loss in weight.

Clarity

The clarity of a diamond is another measure of its value. Collectors and investors continually search for the most perfect stone. As part of that search they are seeking a diamond which is perfectly clear.

Yet few diamonds have such clarity. As part of their formation they frequently contain imperfections called *inclusions*. These inclusions can be from a variety of sources. Usually they come about in the fiery seas below the earth's surface when the diamond crystal is formed. At that time the diamond may be invaded by a parasite crystal of another mineral, such as garnet or olivine. This will typically show up as a bubble in the final diamond. Or there could be an internal (or external) cleavage or even a visible grain line (sometimes called a *growth line*) left over

117

from when the diamond was formed. Other times a flaw may be created in the manufacturing of the diamond.

The list of potential flaws is fairly long and each of them affects the value of the diamond. Naturally the gem that is flawless or nearly so commands the highest price. As the flaws or inclusions increase in severity and number, the price of the diamond goes down. Some commercial diamonds found in jewelry are so heavily flawed that they are called *ice*. In gangster movies, ice normally refers to any diamond. But in the trade, ice refers to a diamond so badly flawed that, when we look into it, it appears like an ice formation. There is virtually no clarity at all, only inclusions. Naturally such stones are on the lower end of the value scale.

The Language of Flaws

In the past there were a number of consumer problems with dealers offering diamonds that were very heavily included, but described in nontechnical terms so that the buyer thought they were near perfect. Perhaps the most common term used to describe a diamond by an unscrupulous dealer was "eye-clean." I suppose that meant that there were lots of inclusions, but they just couldn't be seen—particularly if you weren't an expert and didn't know what to look for.

The term *clean* was so badly abused that eventually the Federal Trade Commission had to step in and ban its use by merchants in the United States. But, disreputable dealers were quick to fill the breach, and they came up with a variety of terms to describe their diamonds. These included everything from "top-grade commercial" to "highest quality."

In response to the need for an industry-wide standard such as had already been established in Europe, the GIA came up with a set of grading criteria for diamond clarity. This grading standard is in use today and is virtually the only grading standard totally accepted by reputable diamond dealers, investors and collectors in the United States. In it the clarity of any diamond can be defined.

The Need for Expert Opinion

The definition, however, is still a matter of expert opinion. For example, a group of tiny spots that can only be seen under a ten-power magnifier could put the diamond into at least two different categories, depending on the size of the spots. Yet it is the eye and brain of the expert that decides how large those spots are, and one expert's opinion may differ from another's.

On some inclusions, there is very little disagreement. But on borderline cases, often there is considerable. At our IDC labs, when there is any disagreement we call in three experts and they discuss it among themselves; all must finally agree before a clarity grade is given.

Microscopic Examination

Another concern with grading is just how carefully we are going to look at the diamond. For example, some flaws that are invisible to the naked eye jump right out at you when the gem is viewed under magnification. Similarly, flaws invisible at five-power magnification become clear at ten-power; those invisible at ten-power jump out at twenty, and so forth. Just how carefully should we search for flaws?

The industry standard calls for an examination under a ten-power lens. A magnification any greater or any less would not meet the standards. However, this creates a new problem. Some minute flaw might indeed be visible under ten-power if we knew it was there. However, it may be very difficult to find if we don't know where to look. To solve this, clarity grading of all diamonds should first be done under sixty-power. Any inclusions noted are then viewed in descending magnification down to ten-power. If they disappear from view, they are then truly not visible under the grading standard. If an inclusion remains visible, then it is a flaw that must be noted. This is the basis for our own *maximum severity analysis*.

There are ten grades that are considered standard in the United States. They are as follows:

Grading Standards for Clarity

FL (FLAWLESS)

This grade is self-defining. Under a ten-power microscope the stone is virtually flawless. I say "virtually" because certain flaws *are* allowed under this grade. For example, on occasion a brillianteerer will discover a slight flaw on one of the facets he is creating. He will then add a minute extra facet to remove the flaw. This may not count against the jewel's perfection. Or, in another example, a flaw could be on the girdle. Because the girdle is the widest part of the diamond, it is the part that is most likely to retain a portion of the rough stone sometimes called the *skin*. On occasion a bit of this skin will be left after bruting. If it in no way interferes with the cut or the gem's ability to refract light, it will not be considered a flaw. Some roughness on the girdle as well as some internal lines, if they don't change the light refracted to the front, are also allowed.

Between the grade of FL and the next lower grade, the *European* market defines an in-between step. This is IF (internally flawless). An internally flawless stone is one that meets from within all the criteria for a flawless stone, but it has some minor cleavage or other problem on the surface, which usually can be remedied by repolishing.

VVS (VERY, VERY SLIGHTLY INCLUDED)

In this grade there are a variety of flaws permissible. The key is that they must be just barely visible when using a ten-power magnifier. In addition, the flaws must not be visible in the table and must all be minor and located at the edges. The VVS is similar to a FL except that the flaws are more easily seen.

There are two grades of VVS. These are listed as:

VVS1

VVS2

The difference between one and two is relatively slight. However it is important, as the price difference between the two grades is significant. Essentially a VVS2 can have the same types of problems that occur in a VVS1, except that in the lower grade they are more pronounced.

VS (VERY SLIGHTLY INCLUDED)

This grade definition allows a broader range of defects including pinpoints (bubbles), some small cracks, scratches, inferior girdle cleavages and lines, all of which may or may not be visible through the table. In general the VS grade has flaws that are not as difficult to find under a ten-power magnifier as with the VVS grade. There are also two grades of VS:

VS1

VS2

As with the VVS, the types of flaws permitted under these two grades are similar. It's just that in the lower grade, the flaws are more severe.

In the past, only the five grades we have just discussed were considered to apply to investment diamonds. Since all are presumably invisible to the naked eye, it is easy to see how false terms such as "clean" could have popped up to deceive the unwary buyer. An unscrupulous dealer might have been selling a VS2 for a FL price and describing both grades as "clean." After all, to the naked eye they would both appear flawless.

Recently, with the reduction in high quality rough coming from the mines and with the increased demand for diamonds, the next two lower grades have come into the investment market. It may be that within a few years, instead of only five top grades considered for investment, there may be seven.

SI (SLIGHTLY INCLUDED)

This category includes a wide variety of problems in the diamond. It can have nicks in the girdle, larger extra facets, bubbles, fissures, structural problems, and even some included crystals of other, darker material. The real test, however, is that these are visible with less than a ten-power microscope. Typically they are visible with a three- to five-power magnifier.

Again, the grade is divided into two categories:

SI1

SI2

These grades have the same criteria except that in the lower grade, once again, the problems with the stone are far more visible. An expert who knows what to look for could probably spot some of the imperfections in an SI2 with the naked eye.

I (IMPERFECT)

This final grade speaks for itself. The inclusions are visible to the naked eye. There are three categories of I diamonds:

I1

I2

I3

Generally speaking, the lower the grade here, the far more visible are the imperfections. These are not investment-grade diamonds.

There is one additional grade of diamond that is sometimes used in the jewelry trade. It is called *rejection* or *pique*. This usually makes up the class of diamonds which I referred to earlier as ice. These are sold to those who want a diamond and don't really care what the quality is. A rejection-grade or an I-grade diamond should never be sold to an investor or a collector of gems.

It really is not possible to truly understand imperfections in diamonds unless you can look at them in a real diamond through a microscope. Even then, to the *untrained eye* an imperfection that would qualify as a VS might be hard to spot in as much as twenty-power magnification! Most imperfections are very difficult to see if you don't know what to look for.

Typically imperfections, shown in Figure 8–5, include *bubbles*, which are usually inclusions of another transparent mineral; *solids*, which are inclusions of a nontransparent material; *clouds*, which are small groupings of the above two; *feathers*, which are tiny cracks that give the appearance of a feather; *cracks*, which are breaks in the stone running against the grain; *grain*, or lines that follow the faces of the octahedron shape; and others.

These, of course, are in addition to all the problems that can occur on the *surface* of the diamond. Many of these were covered under the heading of cut. However, when they are too insignificant to affect the cut grade of a diamond, they may nevertheless affect its clarity, particularly if they change the natural flow of light through the gem. These generally include damage to the girdle, a broken culet, marks left from polishing, scratches, minor cleavages, and pits on the surface.

There is one additional problem that sometimes occurs when two diamonds are carried in the same paper. A paper is the

Figure 8–5

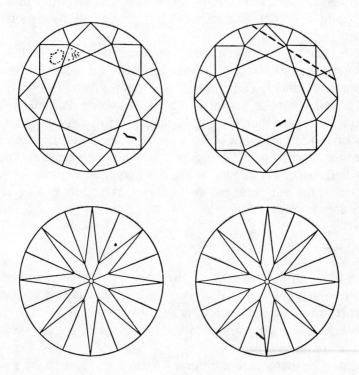

	Internal fracture, feather and hairline feather		External grain, knot or twinning line
	Internal group of pinpoint inclusions		External scratch or wheel mark
	Internal cloud (actual shape)		Internal "carbon" spot

123

traditional method of transporting diamonds. While it may sound strange and even old-fashioned to think of carrying them wrapped in paper, this method has proven its usefulness for centuries.

The paper is folded in a precise manner and once so folded, the diamond cannot escape. You could throw the paper across the room and if it is folded correctly, the diamond will not fall out.

For convenience, sometimes more than one diamond is carried in a single paper. When this happens, the diamonds' natural abrasive qualities work on each other. They tend to scratch one another and become what is termed paper-marked. Paper-marked stones are similar to bag-marked coins that were issued by the mint but damaged en route by having them all packed together in one container.

Color

The final grading criteria is the color of the diamond. Until recently a diamond's color was considered far less important than clarity, cut and carat weight. Over the last few years, however, color has grown in significance because investors became interested in it.

Color in diamonds, strange as it may seem, actually means lack of color. The top-grade diamonds are those that have no color at all. They are generally known as white diamonds.

There are some interesting aspects of color that every diamond buyer should be aware of. The larger the stone, the more likely it is to have some color. This is because the eye recognizes the color more easily in a larger piece. If the large diamond is reduced in size, the color will gradually seem to disappear. Actually, it is lost to the eye through the increased transparency of the tinier jewel.

In the past, color was only judged against pure sunlight. This had to be sunlight from the north in the northern hemisphere, from the south in the southern, and only during the mid-portion of the day. Early in the morning and late at night, sunlight contains too many hues of red and other colors that come from traveling at an angle through the earth's atmosphere. In recent times, however, the light needs for grading has been artificially produced by an instrument called a *colorscope*. It illuminates a small area with pure, white light.

Color Standards

The GIA has established standards for the grading of diamonds that are widely accepted in the United States. The grading standards start with the letter D at the top and run all the way down to the letter Z, the lowest grade. (The reason the GIA didn't start with the obvious letter A was because so many promoters in earlier years used terms such as A or AA or AAA to describe their diamonds. The first letters of the alphabet, therefore, had too many other connotations to be used in a widely accepted color scale.)

Generally speaking, only those grades of color down to the letter I are considered investment diamonds. All other colors are for the jewelry trade and other diamond uses. The reason is simple. To the unaided eye, grades D through H appear colorless or, in the common term, white. Those beginning with the grade I and on down usually have a visible yellowish tinge to them.

Note that I said the "unaided" eye. In grading clarity we use a microscope. But, a magnifier would be of little help here. To grade diamonds for color we use master stones.

Master Stones

Master stones are diamonds that have been expertly graded for color. They consist of at least five diamonds, one each in the various investment grades. To the unaided eye, any one of the master stones would appear white or colorless when considered alone. However, when placed next to each other under the proper light, it immediately becomes apparent that they have a greater degree of color in descending order.

To grade an unknown diamond, the master stones are set a few millimeters apart under a neutral light. Usually the top, or D grade, stone is placed at the left, with the remaining stones set out in descending order to the right. Next the diamond to be graded is brought under the light and placed in turn next to each master stone, beginning at the bottom of the scale. Very quickly the color of the unknown stone will become apparent. By moving it up the scale we will eventually be able to find a master stone that has a clearer color and one which has a deeper color. At that point the unknown stone will be identified. In our lab it will be given the grade of the lower-quality master stone.

While even an inexperienced person can quickly learn to grade diamonds for color by this method, it takes a true expert to be able to see slight differentiations between one grade and another. And only a rare expert, such as Steve Greenbaum, who has an "eye" for diamonds, is able to tell color without using master stones.

Colored Diamonds

In addition to having a yellowish tinge, some diamonds also have other colors. Under a fluorescent light some diamonds fluoresce strong yellow or brown. Some give off a hue which can only be described as blue; diamonds with this property were prized for it at one time. Even today true-blue gems are in demand. However, they are exceedingly rare. Nevertheless, over the years many dealers discovered they could sell their diamonds more easily if they described them as "blues" or "blue whites." The term was so widely used and misused that today no reputable dealer will refer to his stock in terms of a "blue" label.

The Ultimate Guarantee

Ultimately I feel that, when buying a diamond, the same situation applies as when Harry Winston was selling. Certificates are important but when you buy a diamond you also buy a dealer.

As I noted in the earlier chapter on markups, when you buy you should be paying for a professional buyer's having gone to Europe and selected your diamond. Your money should go toward having that diamond brought into the country and having it graded by a reputable lab. The dealer should offer you some education, so you know what you are getting and feel comfortable with it before you buy. The dealer should also have information services to keep you plugged into the market after you purchase. Finally, and most important, the dealer should be big enough so that he can offer you a program of liquidation when you want to sell.

A certificate should be only one facet of an integrated investment program in order for you, the buyer, to be able to sleep comfortably at night with your investment. Remember: *A wise buyer doesn't buy paper. He or she buys diamonds.*

CHAPTER NINE

Protecting Yourself from Fraud

Diamonds are brilliant, they are beautiful and they are profitable—and it is very easy to fall in love with them. Inevitably from time to time unscrupulous people are attracted to the diamond industry because they think they can take advantage of people's emotional reactions to these incredibly beautiful gems, and they aren't much concerned with giving the consumer a square deal. My purpose in this chapter is to alert you to possible problem areas.

I'll deal with some of the villains—as well as some of my own heros—in just a moment. But the first thing a diamond purchaser needs to know is "How do I pick an honest, reliable dealer?"

I have been asked that question so often that I have put together a list to help you discover whether the person you are planning to deal with is legitimate. You may have seen this list, or a shortened version of it, in consumer-advocate newspaper columns. I have encouraged as many people as possible to use it and spread the word. I have no objection to anyone's using my list as long as it helps buyers avoid a bad deal.

Rules for Buying a Diamond

1. *Does the company provide a complete satisfaction money-back guarantee, on product and services, stated in writing?*

If you buy a television set and then find out it doesn't work, you fully expect to be able to take that set back to where you

128

bought it and either have the problem remedied or your money refunded. This is just plain honest treatment due any consumer, and it applies in the diamond industry. If there are any problems, the company you buy your diamond from should be willing to take back the diamond and give you full satisfaction. Always get this assurance in writing. It is just not good enough to take the salesperson's word. If a company is not willing to put its name behind such a guarantee, you should not deal there.

2. *Does the company provide an unconditional written guarantee for the grade and legal description of diamonds delivered?*

There is not a diamond company in America today that doesn't offer a certificate, but just getting a piece of paper isn't enough. You have to read what it says. If the company in any way hedges on its statements of the diamond's grade or seems vague about the diamond's description, stay away! The problem will occur when it is time to sell. Such a company could then reexamine the diamond and down-grade it. The company should be willing to stand by whatever grade it gives the diamond, both when selling it and when liquidating.

3. *Does the firm deliver all diamonds in an unsealed condition suitable for outside examination?*

This covers one of the most outrageous practices I have ever seen. In some cases, grading labs have provided certificates with terrific guarantees. Then they have sealed the diamond in a plastic container and indicated that the guarantees are valid *only* if the container is not broken. This means that you cannot look at the diamond or have an expert examine it. This is an attempt to keep you, the consumer, from fully determining what you have. No reputable diamond lab would mind your having the diamond reexamined. It's the old "sardines in a can" story. It could be that when you finally break the seal and look at the diamond, it is not at all what the certificate says it is.

Please keep in mind that *diamonds are unique*. If you have a precise legal description of a diamond, you could take that stone and drop it into a pile of 10,000 other stones of the same weight. It might take some time but, using that description, eventually a good lab would be able to pick out your diamond again. Having the container open does not mean that you can switch one dia-

129

mond for another or that any good lab is worried about that. It means that the lab is confident enough about its judgement not to care whether you or anyone else takes a second look.

4. *Does the company provide a corporate resume on the operational history of the firm, including third-party financial references?*

Jewelers have been selling diamonds to consumers for hundreds of years in this country. But it is a relatively new phenomenon amongst investment firms. Therefore, to be sure that the firm you are dealing with is not a fly-by-night outfit, you should check its references. Any reputable company will not mind this— in fact, they will encourage it. Also, you should not simply rely on the company's statements. Use third-party reports to confirm what the company says.

5. *Does the company provide an unpressured opportunity for you to study the market and carefully select the best combination of service and value from an educated position?*

Diamonds are forever. That means, in part, that you don't have to buy, in fact you shouldn't buy, the first time you are offered one. Ideally the person selling you the diamond will first educate you about diamonds. In fact, the person selling you the stone should only give you information on the field. Once you have the appropriate information, you will be able to make a sound judgement entirely on your own.

I am concerned about salespeople who use high-pressure tactics, trying to force the customer to buy through intimidation. If you feel pressured to make a purchase, you are dealing with the wrong person. A reputable company will want your longterm business. Therefore they will never pressure you to make a quick decision.

Along these same lines, you should never buy a diamond, or agree to buy one, over the phone (unless it is from a dealer with whom you have dealt before, whom you personally know and trust).

There are some salespeople who simply sit in a room and make hundreds of phone calls trying to dig up business. There is nothing wrong with a salesperson calling to ask for the opportunity to meet you and explain the diamond field. There is something very wrong with a salesperson calling to tell you he has a hot deal on a stone, but only if you act within the next twenty minutes!

6. *Does the company furnish an independent Certified Public Accountant's audited statement of past performance for previous diamond investors?*

You want to deal with a winner, not a loser. You also want to be sure you are not the first person to whom this company has sold a diamond. The best way to be assured of this is to take a look at the company's past performance. I am not talking about how many diamonds they have sold to other people. I am talking about how many they've *liquidated* (bought back) and how much profit their clients made.

A reputable company will be happy to show you its track record. What could please the firm more than to have you, the consumer, see how well other clients have done? If the company doesn't have an audited statement of its track record, stay away. I would also be wary of any company that had not done at least several million dollars in the aftermarket.

7. *Does the company provide a financial report to diamond owners on changes in selling prices for diamonds acquired?*

When you buy a diamond from an investment company, you should be asking for a whole series of services. One of these is an updating system to keep you informed of what is happening in the field. After all, you have made an investment. It would be strange if you were not concerned about how your investment was doing from moment to moment. And who would be better able to tell you than the company from which you made your purchase?

A reputable company will provide continual updating on any changes in selling prices as well as on the diamond market in general. These should be *original* reports created by the company's own investigative staff, not simply reprints from a magazine or newspaper article.

8. *Does the company operate locally, with fulltime service personnel in your home community?*

When you make an investment, the last thing you want to do is to buy from someone who is going to leave the area next week. You want to buy from a person who is a member of your community, who has roots. This is a person you can go back to in case there's a problem later on. You also want a person who can advise you on future investments.

There's a reason the term *fly-by-night* came into existence. It means a salesperson sells during the day and flees during the night. It means that the product he or she is selling has a *problem*.

On the other hand, someone who is a solid member of your community has a reputation to maintain. He or she is going to see to it *personally* that you get a fair deal.

9. *Does the company have a minimum five-year operating history in the market?*

Diamond dealers come and go, but the reputable companies last. For one way to determine just how good the company you're dealing with is, take a look at how long it has been in business. Since diamonds investment companies are still fairly new in this country, you are not going to find one that has been around for half a century. Be sure that the company has been in the diamond business for at least five years.

10. *Does the company belong to reputable and established trade associations in the diamond industry?*

This only makes common sense. The minimum here would be the Jewelers Board of Trade and the Chamber of Commerce; other trade or consumer organizations would be a plus. If the company cannot muster participation in these groups, then there must be a good reason, and you would be wise not to stick around to find out.

These ten rules will help you find a reputable dealer or investment firm. In addition, I have four more for when it comes time to sell.

11. *Is a stone quotation provided?*

This may seem simple-minded, but it really isn't. Some dealers will simply agree to buy and then send you a check. You want to know up front what they are offering to pay so that you can compare it with other dealers. As I mentioned when discussing the aftermarket, you should get at least five quotes from diamond dealers.

12. *Is a gross sales price and a liquidation value disclosed without obligation?*

When you are selling, it is helpful to know how much you are getting and how much the dealer is getting. If it turns out that the dealer is getting more than you, you know there is something fishy. A reputable dealer will give figures on the gross value of the diamond as well as the amount you are getting and the amount he is getting for handling the transaction.

13. *Are all fees and charges fully disclosed?*

Some dealers will say they are going to sell your diamond and take back only 2 or 3 percent for themselves. But when all is done you may find that in addition to the small 2 or 3 percent commission, there are fees and charges that mount up to 50 percent or more of what you thought you would get!

You should determine initially if there are any fees and charges in addition to the dealer's commission. If there are, you should know the amounts as closely as possible. It's the only way you can truly know what you are getting.

14. *Is the discount off current selling price disclosed in writing to the consumer without obligation?*

What is critical here is the statement "in writing." If you are going to go around to several dealers to get quotes, you want to be sure that these dealers will honor their quotes. One may say that he will give you top dollar. Then when you come back his price suddenly drops. If, however, he has given you his quote in writing, it is not likely to change. It makes determining the sales price a whole lot safer for you.

I cannot guarantee that these fourteen rules will get you a good investment or a good dealer, but they should send you a long way in the right direction. I have some other advice of a general nature that can help keep you out of trouble. Much of what follows I learned through my own experience.

Diamond Investment Pitfalls

THE SELF-MADE "EXPERT"

I feel that I am qualified to speak on diamonds. I helped create the largest diamond import brokerage firm in the world and currently remain instrumental in its operation and policies. I spend perhaps a third of each year outside of the country, and I talk with international banks in France, England, Belgium, Israel and other countries. On occasion I speak personally with world leaders. I consider these minimum credentials for writing a book to give advice on economics and diamonds. When I speak on the subject, it is from personal experience.

I have been appalled by the number of pseudo-experts who have crawled out of the woodwork in recent years. The "experts" I'm talking about have had no success in business or elsewhere. In most cases they have had little or no economic background. They have had almost no personal experiences that they could use to show why anyone should believe what they are saying. I'll never understand how they made the decision to become an expert.

These people (and I'm sure you've either read their books or heard them speak) sometimes begin by saying that they started off broke and starving and that they were previously failures. Then people started giving them money, and today they are millionaires. Tracing the progress of their careers, I find they usually started making money when they started giving advice. It was their books and their speaking engagements and in some cases their newsletters that made them wealthy.

I really do not understand why people would want to take advice from failures. Perhaps it is the case that if someone is brash enough to stand up and give advice, many people are inclined to listen—to even pay for the privilege of listening.

The truly unfortunate part of all this is the track record of such "experts." Over the years I've observed that most of the advice and predictions of these pseudo-economists are wrong. Their recommendations for buying products have a horrible track record. What really bothers me is that I see some of these people recommending that the public buy diamonds.

Perhaps that seems odd, since I earn my livelihood from marketing diamonds. But it isn't strange at all. These "experts" have made recommendations in the diamond field that are awful. They tell their listeners what to buy and how to buy and it results in terrible losses. It gives the entire diamond field a bad name.

My suggestion here is to check the credentials of the person to whom you are listening. There are simple questions to ask. Ask this person "How much money have you made in diamonds? How big a company do you own? What entitles you to speak on the subject?" If the "expert's" credentials are only poverty and failure, I would think twice about listening to his or her advice.

DON'T BELIEVE A DIAMOND "INDEX"

There's no such thing as a "paper diamond." We discussed that concept with regard to certificates, but even more important is its use with regard to pricing. The whole point is that diamonds are unique, no two are alike. They have intrinsic value based upon discriminations of their ability to transmit colorless light back to the eye in a shower of refracted colors at maximum purity. Since no two diamonds are alike, it is impossible to give an overall price for diamonds. *No index for diamonds is possible!* Yet I know that some companies right off the bat give you a price list for diamonds. They say a given category of diamonds are this price today, were that price yesterday and will be another price tomorrow. Some even advertise their index price. Consumers have to be wary of such companies. Frequently the price such companies charge for their diamonds is based on the index. And that makes no sense.

When an honest diamond company calculates the price of a diamond it sells, the calculation is made on the basis of cost. The firm knows what it paid, what its expenses are, and what profit it can expect to receive and still stay competitive. That is how jewelers sell diamonds. That is how any reputable investment company sells diamonds. To base the price of a particular grade of diamond not on the factors of cost, expenses and competitive profit, but instead on some arbitrary index would make little sense unless the company planned to use that index to boost the price and take advantage of the consumer.

I would be wary of any diamond dealer who quotes an indexed price of diamonds. Chances are that dealer may be trying to create a speculative fever in the field and generate quick-money business.

ADVERTISED DISCOUNT DIAMOND PRICES

Every so often I see ads in the paper offering to buy (or sometimes sell) diamonds at what is called a "discount" price. I can tell you that there is no such thing as a "diamond discount price." Occasionally, rarely, in a very slow market, someone— usually an individual who must sell quickly—will take less than a diamond is worth just to liquidate it fast. Usually, it is only the diamond wholesaler who is in a position to take advantage of such bargains. This dealer is the one who is approached and who normally makes the purchase. For an investor or consumer to find such a situation is like finding the proverbial needle in a haystack.

Out of curiosity I have answered ads for discount diamonds. Invariably when I get very specific, asking for grades of color and clarity, weight and the proportion of cut, things get a little fuzzy on the seller's end.

More likely than not, such a dealer is actually charging more than market price, hoping that the buyer simply does not know what a diamond should cost. And when you are selling, such a dealer may actually be offering less, again playing on the seller's ignorance. But, if it turns out that his price *is* a discount from the market, invariably the dealer is selling a certificate. Because the certificate says the diamond is a particular grade and he is offering it at a price less than that grade dictates, it is supposedly a discount. When the actual diamond is examined, however, we may find it is a lower grade—hence no real discount was achieved.

Certificates

My company puts out a certificate that we recognize as authoritative. We honor the grade that is on it, but we do *not* honor the grade on any other laboratory's certificate. Nobody honors the grade on another company's certificate. (Many companies won't even honor the grade on their own certificate!) Buying only a certificate and not a company can mean problems.

The European Gemological Laboratories (EGL) is a well-known lab in Europe with a great deal of credibility. Yet, we recently did a survey. We took diamonds that had EGL certificates and then regraded them in our labs. The results of this random sampling were surprising. In 6 out of 10 cases, our grade was different from that of EGL. In approximately 70 percent of those cases we graded lower and in 30 percent we graded higher than EGL.

Does that mean that the EGL is a bad lab? Not at all. It is an excellent lab. It's just that grading is ultimately an art form—a statement of opinion. And the grading standards of the EGL are somewhat different from our own. The same holds true for standards of the GIA or any other lab. No lab or certificate provides an ultimate grade. It all depends on what the buyer and seller are willing to accept.

The problem comes about when an investor buys a diamond with a certificate and then tries to resell. Is that investor going to be able to resell at the stated grade on the certificate, or will the new buyer demand a new evaluation and, potentially, a new grade? If there is even a difference of one grade down, it could have a devastating effect on the price. A "bargain" on purchase, could turn into a disaster on sale.

Lack of Consumer Action on Frauds

If I thought I had been cheated in buying a diamond, you can bet that I would howl. I would want the company that cheated me put out of business right now. But it's amazing the number of consumers who simply write off their loss to experience and do nothing about it.

Today there is virtually no regulation of certificates. Almost anybody can set up a lab and issue certificates, so it is up to the buyer to know the good labs from the fly-by-night outfits.

On the other hand, the Federal Trade Commission does make some effort to regulate the advertising of diamonds. Certain words are forbidden. For example, a dealer can't use the word *perfect*. We cannot use the word *flawless* unless certain criteria are met. We cannot use the term *well-proportioned*, which we use in investment-grade diamonds, unless a diamond has certain characteristics. The term *blue-white*, which we discussed earlier, is also outlawed. Any person who uses these terms in advertising is subject to action by the Federal Trade Commission. Any consumer who was cheated because of relying on these words should contact the Commission and demand action.

Beyond that, any consumer who was cheated or even suspects he or she was cheated should contact the local District Attorney's office. The D.A. in each city is set up to receive such complaints and check them out. In some cases, a complaint to the D.A. may result in the consumer's getting back some of the money that was lost. He won't stop those few unscrupulous dealers unless the consumer acts.

Beware of These Villains

This next section I like to call the villains in the diamond industry. These are companies which have caused great harm from a wide variety of sources. Fortunately most are now out of business. Unfortunately, some are starting up again, often under the same name in new areas. If you see them, watch out.

DeBEERS DIAMOND INVESTMENT, LTD.

DeBeers is the name given to the DeBeers syndicate which as we've seen in previous chapters controls about 80 percent of the diamond rough in the world.

DeBeers Diamond Investment, Ltd. is a company that was originally located in Phoenix, Arizona. *DeBeers Diamond Investment, Ltd. has nothing to do with the DeBeers syndicate.*

DeBeers Diamond Investment, Ltd. sold not only diamonds, but also colored gemstones. They sold merchandise in sealed plastic, bait-and-switch containers. I suspect that not that many people purchased with them, but there was harmful publicity. The DeBeers syndicate has spent countless millions creating an image of stability in the diamond field, and all of a sudden this firm from Arizona adopted a similar name and the goodwill that had been created over the years began to go down the drain.

In the United States it is unlikely that the consumer would buy directly from DeBeers; the consumer would buy from a jeweler or an investment company. Therefore, if the company you're buying from has the name *DeBeers* on it, be very careful.

DIAMOND QUOTE

There was a man in Newport Beach, California, who recently operated a firm called *Diamond Quote*. He quoted diamond prices every day. Usually the prices quoted were so far below the market, that it was unbelievable. He advertised heavily in major publications.

Now, there is nothing wrong with selling below market value, except that this company *promised* liquidation and the ability for people to plug back into the market. The company, however, simply didn't have it.

We wrote this company letters. We wanted them to stop. We thought that they were cheating the consumer. In turn, they said horrible things about almost every other diamond company in the field.

So what happened? Today the company is gone. The owner went to Brazil and those who bought at the Diamond Quote prices don't have the original outlet for their diamonds.

American Association of Diamond Merchants

Another organization that in my opinion spread more harm than good was the American Association of Diamond Merchants (AADM). This was a trade group that was set up, we thought, to establish ethics in the business. The truth of the matter was that it was formed by a man who owned a diamond company. He would take inquiries from the public and then try to sell diamonds right on the telephone. These diamonds were from his own diamond investment sales company.

Worse than that, in my estimation, he would give out bad information on others in the trade and on other diamond companies. He used the AADM to build his own name.

Many companies were taken in by the AADM at first. When it first opened, we thought it was a good idea. We were in favor of anyone or any organization that would build ethics. We were gullible and donated thousands of dollars to it, becoming a sponsor. It appeared to be a good organization.

Ultimately, the very members of AADM caused it to be disbanded.

Diamond Dealers of New York

The New York Diamond Dealers Club has thousands of members in the wholesale diamond trade and represents billions in diamond trades each year. You would expect these dealers to be reputable, simply because of the organization to which they belong. My concern with them has to do with the fact that some of these people are advertising an "inter-dealer price index." It sounds like they are advertising a *world market price* (or an index, or a ticker tape, or an "official" price) for a given diamond.

It is impossible to give a single true market price. Yet some of the New York Diamond Dealers put one out every day based on what they term their "survey." How big is this survey? What are the statistics? I have never seen them published. Yet I pick up a prestigious paper such as *The Wall Street Journal* and see "Inter-dealer," the New York Diamond Dealer price. What does it mean? If I don't know, how can the consumer?

My company puts out a diamond bluebook that is much in demand by jewelers and dealers. It comes out every quarter and lists 50,000 prices—wholesale, investor, retail for many different levels. Right in the book we specify that our prices may or may not have any resemblance to actual world market conditions. We acknowledge that grading standards vary and diamonds are so individual that there simply is no single world price. Our book may be a helpful appraiser's guideline, but even with 50,000 prices it is not an index for world market prices.

There is a bluebook that is used for giving automobile prices. It lists thousands of prices for cars both new and used. But would anyone in their wildest imagination conclude that there is one U.S. price for mid-size cars, compacts, full-size luxury cars? If people aren't foolish enough to believe such a thing of the automobile industry, why should they believe it of the diamond industry?

I have seen the same New York Dealers raise their index on certain types of diamonds when there has been no market rise at all. In my opinion, that's an artificial attempt to sell diamonds. I have seen them lower the index when the market has not gone down. They have used percentages that have no relationship, in my opinion, to the real market.

I believe the diamond dealer clubs, New York and elsewhere, should impose on their membership a policy where the dignity of the club and its membership restricts advertising on prices except for inventory on hand that a member will actually sell at the prices listed. As a corollary, any prices that represent inventory other than what a member possesses for sale must have a disclaimer indicating that they are not representative of any particular mean average index value or global market condition for diamond prices, but are estimates by the members only.

A Good Guy

Having thus voiced my gripes about several organizations, let me point out one that I think has established a very handsome record for performance. That company is *Innovative Diamond Company* of Orange County, California. This is a responsible company that has a record of concern for the consumer, and they advertise their track record.

Manmade Substitutes

I want to talk about synthetic and simulated diamonds here, not because there is anything wrong with creating them, but because I am concerned with how they are being advertised and, in some cases, sold in the marketplace.

First, let's differentiate between the two types of man-made creations. A *simulated* diamond is not a true diamond: It is not as hard, doesn't have the same brilliance and has a different crystalline structure. To the unaided eye of a nonexpert, however, a simulated diamond may appear to be the real thing.

A *synthetic*, on the other hand, is a true diamond. However, instead of being made by nature over thousands of years, it was made by man in a few hours. Those interested in purchasing diamonds for investment are always curious about synthetics. What would happen to the value of diamonds if investment-quality synthetics suddenly were produced for a few cents, particularly if they were produced in such quality that no one could tell them from the real investment diamonds?

The answer to this concern is "Don't worry." Millions of synthetic diamonds are produced annually, yet almost none even approximates investment quality. This has to do with the physical requirements for creating a synthetic stone. To produce a synthetic, man must come close to duplicating nature. That means creating a vessel or capsule capable of containing incredible heat and pressure. (The heat is often close to 3000 degrees and the pressure is as high as 100,000 atmospheres!) It is possible to do this, and the first synthetics were produced in the early 1950s simultaneously in Europe and by the General Electric Company in the United States. Since that time the Russians have developed their own process, as has the DeBeers syndicate.

The important point is that virtually all synthetics have been in the lowest grades, suitable only for industrial uses such as oil drill bits or other hard cutting surfaces.

In the entire world there have only been about a dozen or so synthetic diamonds that approached a grade high enough to warrant consideration as investment diamonds. (Remember, even in natural stones, investment grade diamonds represent only about one percent of the total diamond harvest.)

Cheap Diamond Ads

In recent years I have noticed ads in top publications to the effect that, if you send in $5.95 or $10.95 or some other ridiculously low figure, you will be sent back a "genuine, authentic" diamond. I do not think that anyone reading this book would be foolish enough to answer this ad, but many of you may be curious about it. No doubt what is being purchased is a true diamond, an industrial grade stone, probably a synthetic. I suspect that if the buyer pays $10 for the stone, its true worth is probably one dollar or less.

This is about as close to the investment market as synthetics get. Those who are concerned that synthetics may someday flood the market for investment stones need a good course in physics. There are natural laws that cannot be broken. Heat and pressure cannot be created easily nor can substitutes be found for them. It truly takes a caldron such as exists beneath the earth's crust to make flawless diamonds.

Simulated Stones

Simulated stones can in no way be considered real diamonds, but they have certain properties that make them appear similar to diamonds.

YAG

The first product to appear in the marketplace that was a true simulated diamond (beyond the glass or paste used before and easily recognized) was the YAG (yttrim aluminate). It is sold under a variety of trade names, but is always referred to by the three letters of its chemical name.

The YAG has properties similar to those of a real diamond. It is fairly hard. On the MOHs scale, which measures hardness on a range of 1 to 10, diamonds, being the hardest substance known, rate a 10. A YAG falls somewhere between 8 and 9. A YAG is also capable of being cut and polished in a fashion similar to a diamond. It is possible to create a near-perfect 58-facet round brilliant cut with a YAG.

YAGs, however, have less than half the brilliance and fire of a diamond. They look like a diamond at first glance, but they don't glimmer as much. Even the unaided eye of a nonexpert can quickly tell a YAG given a few moments to examine it. YAGs are used almost exclusively for jewelry. Typically a person will buy a real diamond, and a similarly cut YAG. On those occasions when the owner is wearing jewelry in public and there is fear of theft, the YAG is substituted for the diamond. The cost of YAG is very low. A one-carat YAG can be purchased for about $50 or less.

There are other similar simulated diamond materials including strontium titanate and synthetic rutile. Strontium titanate is very soft and cannot be faceted very well. Synthetic rutile has a definite yellowish cast. Both these are sometimes used as simulated diamonds, but rarely in recent years.

Cubic Z

Perhaps the best simulated stone to be created is a product known as zirconium oxide or, by its more common name, Cubic Z.

Cubic Z entered the marketplace in the late 1970s and was hailed as a true diamond substitute. It is available in either a colorless stone or in a wide variety of colors that can be added at the time it is manufactured. It is hard enough to withstand faceting and it has a refractive index close to diamond so that it seems to be as brilliant unless closely examined. When cut and placed into a setting such as jewelry, it can easily deceive the nonexpert.

When it was first introduced, Cubic Z was sold by some unscrupulous people as a real diamond. Reports circulated that even jewelers could not tell it apart. For a time some people thought that a true, inexpensive synthetic diamond had been created. (A one-carat Cubic Z stone actually costs less in many cases than a YAG.) Nothing could be further from the truth. Any jeweler can tell a Cubic Z without even examining it. Simply wetting one's finger and lifting the Cubic Z informs the observer that it is not diamond. A diamond cannot be wetted, but a Cubic Z adheres to water.

Flaws Manufactured with Cubic Z

What is remarkable about a Cubic Z is that it can be manufactured to have many of the flaws, such as feathers, cracks and cleavages, that appear in true diamonds. In our labs, I have seen jokes played on our technical experts when a Cubic Z, flawed, is included with a group of real diamonds. The expert immediately notices that the refractive properties are different, as is the size-to-weight ratio. But the flaws are there. After a few moments of puzzlement, the expert invariably rises from the microscope to search for the prankster who is wasting his time.

A Cubic Z never has been and never will be a true diamond. It is simply costume jewelry. Placed in a nice setting it can satisfy many of those who see it. But the owner always knows it isn't real.

Beware of bargain diamonds sold at ridiculously low prices— they could be Cubic Z. Another test to tell if the stone is a true diamond or a Cubic Z is the breath test. This is particularly helpful when the piece is in a setting and cannot be easily examined. Warm breath blown over a diamond contains a great deal of moisture. Yet, because water does not adhere to a true diamond, no mist will form on it. The opposite is true of Cubic Z. Nevertheless, the best guarantee of getting a true diamond is to buy your stone from a reputable jeweler or investment company.

"Improved" Diamonds

One last area of consumer concern has to do with real diamonds that have been "improved." It has been discovered that exposing a diamond to gamma radiation for example, will change it to a deep green color. Heating of diamonds to about 1500 degrees F, on the other hand, will change the stone to yellow or brown. While none of these techniques can be used to remove color and thus improve quality, they have been used to create a range of interesting colored diamonds. In both cases, however, the color is only "skin deep." It can be polished off the surface.

Attempts to change the color of a diamond (actually, to remove color) have mostly been fraudulent acts. Over the years a wide variety of techniques have been employed, including painting on the surface of the stone or putting a slight violet mark at some point on the pavillion to counteract the yellow of the diamond, making it appear more bluish. All these techniques have been aimed at convincing a buyer that a particular diamond is something more than it really is. Fortunately, experts can tell fairly easily if something has been colored on the surface.

Laser Treatment

One technique that is fairly new has been used in a number of cases we have uncovered at our lab. The diamond has been treated with a laser to improve either clarity or color. It works in this fashion. A minute hole is laser-cut into the diamond to the site of an inclusion. The inclusion is then either filled or removed making the diamond appear clearer. Similarly, laser holes have been drilled into stones and then color has been leached out. Laser treating of diamonds is not something that a nonexpert can normally spot, but an expert examining a diamond under a microscope can quickly see the trail left by the laser hole, even when it has been filled.

Laser treating of diamonds does sometimes improve their

value. The laser hole, of course, detracts from the grade of the diamond. But if the laser hole detracts less than the large inclusion or the bad color that was removed, the stone truly has been improved. Laser treatment is normally done only with lowest quality stones and is at best only a hit-or-miss technique.

In this chapter I've tried to outline some of the areas that a consumer should be wary of when purchasing a diamond. If I've given you any one thought to take away, I hope it is that you should always deal with a reputable firm. A non-expert looking for a bargain diamond is the worst kind of sucker.

Diamond Heros

There are far more good companies in the business than bad and I would be painting an inaccurate picture if I only depicted those that gave the consumer problems. There are also good dealers, and I want to indicate several who are my heros in diamonds.

The first is Harry Winston. Winston was a New York diamond dealer who lived during the Great Depression and the period of enormous growth after the Second World War. He was renowned in American society as *the* American diamond dealer. His slogan was something to the effect that if you wanted a diamond for a quarter-million dollars or less, he couldn't really help you — but if you wanted a diamond for half a million or more, his was the only house in the world.

Winston gave to the diamond industry one of the most extraordinary gifts that has ever been imparted. He gave diamonds magnificence. He sold the largest, finest and most expensive stones probably ever sold by one source in the history of the world. He gave the Hope diamond as well as dozens of others to the Smithsonian. Traveling back and forth across the Atlantic, he would frequently have precious diamonds stuffed in papers in the pockets of his coat.

Winston had perhaps the most unusual perspective of any person in the diamond industry. He was an expert's expert. He knew diamonds in the rough and at every stage of cutting. Even into his seventies he loved every aspect of his trade and what the diamond meant for human beings. There have been other great figures in the diamond industry such as Laszare Kaplan who was a cutter, a legendary figure. But Harry Winston was the premier diamond dealer. Even his name became synonymous with diamonds. When Elizabeth Taylor or other celebrities wanted to buy, it wasn't enough that they simply buy diamonds—they had to be Harry Winston diamonds.

After Harry Winston, if I had a hero in the diamond industry, it would be Steve Greenbaum. Steve is little-known outside the diamond industry, although I have mentioned elsewhere in this book that he was a pioneer in establishing the concept of diamond certificates. Steve has done things that have made him a bit of a celebrity in the industry, but, because he generally does not get involved in the big stones like Winston sold, he has not gained fame outside.

Steve decided to sell diamonds when he was only about nineteen years old and working his way through college. He is still a relatively young man, yet he has global diamond buying teams working for him. He is recognized and has friends in the diamond industry in Israel, London, New York, Antwerp—virtually every diamond capital you could name. Steve, perhaps more than anyone else, worked to build an IBM-like diamond company from nothing but dreams and imagination and honesty and integrity.

Even today some of the diamond greats from around the world, people far older than Steve, will send diamonds to him for his opinion. They seek out his judgement because he has a great asset that no one can learn and no one can buy. Steve has one of the greatest "eyes" for diamonds in the world today.

I can still vividly recall when his grandfather, Jack Serin, who was over seventy years old at the time, stood in front of our brand new IDC world-headquarters building at opening ceremonies. It was four stories tall, covered over 30,000 square feet and overlooked five other buildings housing various groups of the company. When Jack stood in front of the building to cut the red ribbon at the opening ceremony, he had four generations of family there—family whose business was the diamond industry.

He looked out over the crowd and said "I want to tell you people what built this company and what is important in this company, because without this, there would be no building and we would not be here today. What's important in this company is two words, Steven Greenbaum, my grandson. The reason is because he has two things without which you cannot make what he has done in the company come true. First, he has the eye. Second, he has the integrity. This is my grandson in whom I am well pleased."

It's not hard to see why I regard Steve as a hero.

CHAPTER TEN

Best Buy Recommendations

I truly believe that diamonds are the best possible investment in the world. My family owns no other investment. We own no stocks, no bonds, no big savings accounts, and no real estate, with the exception of the house in which we live. We haven't bought anything except diamonds, and we own as many diamonds as we can afford.

"You're not very diversified," I have heard people comment when I mention our investment. "Quite the contrary," I point out. We are exceedingly well-diversified. We diversified within diamonds.

Diamond Mutual Funds

I consider diamonds to be the mutual funds of the twenty-first century. Please note I said *funds*, plural. I have bought into the equivalent of many mutual funds with this precious gem.

To understand what diversification within diamonds means, and why that is the key to buying them, let's for a moment review some diamond basics. As we know by now, diamonds are unique. But there are certain broad categories of diamonds, the easiest of which to understand is weight. If we consider the weight of diamonds, we find that they are not bought and sold randomly; rather there are a number of distinct markets. It is these markets that I call the diamond mutual funds.

Melee as Investment

Let's consider melee. Recall that melee are diamonds whose carat weight is generally 0.25 carats (25 points) and under. These are the very small diamonds.

Even today it is still possible to buy melee diamonds in investment grades for only a few hundred dollars. But aren't melee too small to appreciate in value? We have all heard of those huge diamonds such as the Hope or the Cullinan whose principle claim to fame was their size. Now we are talking about the very smallest of diamonds. We know that the price of diamonds goes up almost geometrically with their size. How can we say that melee are suitable diamonds for investment purposes?

The melee market is the largest single market for diamonds. There are perhaps more melee than all other diamonds put together. When you get a diamond ring that contains more than a single stone, chances are you've bought melee. There may be a large stone in the center, but there will be melee surrounding it.

Melee are used to make up diamond earrings and broaches and pendants. They are the basic diamonds of jewelry. They are used to add fire to the large stones—to give the jewelry the appearance of having a much larger diamond within.

Melee, small though they are, aspire to be perfect cut diamonds. Gem melee have 58 facets just like the bigger stones. They are graded like the bigger stones. (In today's market melee are strictly graded, but a decade ago many were not.) Melee are diamonds of a caliber comparable to larger stones, the major difference being that they are smaller.

Since melee are used so extensively in jewelry, they do make up the biggest single market for diamonds. And since their market is so large, there is always a demand for melee. This means that the person who owns melee has bought into a market which has enormous volume. You can always buy or sell melee even when other diamonds may not be moving.

I refer to melee as a diamond mutual fund. The price of melee, as well as other diamonds, has gone upward. In fact, melee as a group probably has been the fastest growing of all diamond mutual funds. Between 1970 and 1979 the greatest growth over all other size combinations was in melee. It outpaced the bigger stones!

Melee, therefore, offers price appreciation as well as volume. For an investor in diamonds not to consider melee would be a serious mistake. On the other hand, for an investor to put all of his or her money into melee might be an equally big mistake.

Half-Carat Market

There is another category of investment diamonds made up of stones ranging in size around half a carat. This includes diamonds that are up to three-quarters of a carat and down to a quarter-carat, but the average size is about half a carat.

Earlier in this book I noted that 4 out of 5 brides in the United Stats received a diamond engagement ring. The ratio is as high in Europe and slightly higher in Japan. These diamonds are bought not so much for their investment potential (although I am sure that is always considered) as for their romantic appeal. Statistics indicate that the vast majority of the diamonds bought for brides are in the half-carat range. They are somewhat larger than melee, but still smaller than one carat. The half-carat stone, therefore, is another diamond mutual fund.

There will always be a demand for the half-carat stone, at least as long as there are brides. Jewelers are interested in them, and they buy and sell many half-carat diamonds (as they do melee). In fact, the investment-grade diamonds that we are likely to find in jewelry stores are the half-carat and melee variety. Jewelers tend not to carry the larger stones.

What is the difference between the half-carat mutual fund and the melee mutual fund? They appreciate at different rates and at different times. They are ultimately different markets. What this means is that, while half-carat stones may be sitting still in terms of price for a year or longer, melee may be moving up. Similarly, while melee may be dormant, the half-carat stones may be moving.

The One-Carat Mutual Fund

Another mutual fund is that of one-carat stones. This fund does not have nearly the volume of the others we've discussed, but it does have price. One-carat stones (by which I mean diamonds that are between three-quarters carat and almost two-carat) are generally bought by more mature buyers. They are the diamonds that are purchased for diamond anniversaries and by families who have achieved a certain amount of wealth through their life. They are also purchased by investors.

Once again, the one-carat mutual fund does not move at the same time or the same rate as the half-carat or the melee funds. It moves at its own rate. It may be taking a giant step forward, while the others are standing still. Or the reverse may be true.

Collector Diamonds

Finally, there is the mutual fund that involves the big stones, over two-carat and up. These are, generally speaking, the investor/collector stones. They are fantastically expensive and they are very limited in supply. It is usually this mutual fund that people speak of when they talk about the diamond market. They are really talking about the big, famous stones. They may have seen an announcement that at an auction somewhere, prices were realized that were 200 or 500 percent over what diamonds were bought for just a few years earlier. "The diamond market must be hot now," is a typical comment. Actually, it's the two-carat and larger mutual fund that is hot. The rest of the diamond market may be booming as well, or course, or it could be quiet.

I think a large disservice to the diamond field comes when in these widely publicized sales a diamond in this category had been sold at little or no appreciation. Quite often such a sale will make the papers, and ill-advised commentators will conclude from it that the diamond market is standing still.

At this point I and my colleagues usually have our hands full explaining why this widely publicized information is incorrect. Our explanation, of course, is that the market for larger diamonds may indeed not be moving. But that in no way means that the market for other diamonds is standing still. At the same time the market for melee could be shooting off the charts, as happened at least once during the 1970s. It is like concluding that because Cadillacs or Mercedes aren't selling, the whole automobile field is dead. It could be that economy Fords and Chevies are breaking sales records.

There are, of course, other more specific types of mutual funds within diamonds, but I think that the four I've outlined here are a good beginning: melee, half-carat, one-carat and larger stones.

Diamond Categories Are Almost Endless

At this point, we have to backtrack just a bit. We have emphasized that diamonds are unique—that each stone is a miniature Rembrandt. This holds true within each of these four mutual funds. Within the half-carat fund, for example, there are numerous grades for color, for clarity and even for cut. Therefore, within the greater half-carat mutual fund, there are lots of different little mutual funds. These are for different grades, and operate independently. VVS stones may be moving while VS are fairly slow—all within the half-carat range. The same could hold true for different grades of color. Or buyers may be demanding less perfect cuts, so those stones closer to the perfect cut are not appreciating as fast.

I point this out here to be sure that it is understood that the four mutual funds I've outlined are really quite general. There is room for diversification within these fields as well.

Diversity for Maximum Appreciation and Safety

Having said that, let me explain why it is so important to understand the concept of mutual funds in diamonds. I use the term *mutual fund* because I think it has a special meaning for most Americans. For years, stock-market mutual funds were considered *the* place to put investment money. Why? Because the value of these funds increased year after year. Stock prices went up and so did the portfolio value of investors. Over the course of time, mutual funds began to take on a new meaning. They meant, not simply a grouping of stocks, but something that always went up in value. The words came to mean more than was originally intended.

It is a bit of both of these meanings that I use here. Like stocks, I mean a diversified investment—a portfolio that isn't just one company, but many. I also mean something that continues to go up in value.

When I speak of diamond mutual funds I mean diversity and appreciation. Now, which diamond mutual fund should you buy?

I've already listed four mutual funds according to weight. There are dozens and dozens more ranging according to the other grades. Which ones makes the most sense as an investment? The question is "If I want to buy diamonds, what should I buy?"

My answer is buy a diverse group of diamonds. Buy from a lot of different mutual funds.

If someone comes to me and says they want to invest in diamonds, I almost never tell them to invest in only one stone. (The only times I would suggest a single diamond investment is if they either had very little money or they had a very specific and limited investment objective.) I tell them to diversify, to spread their investment out in the four mutual funds I've mentioned and, if they have enough money, to then invest in the various grades within these mutual funds.

My reasoning should be apparent. Part of the reason for putting money in diamonds is so that they can be used as a "God forbid" account. There may come a day in the future when a certain portion of the investment must be liquidated quickly. There could be a medical emergency, sickness in the family, or someone could be out of work. Whatever the reason, the need for money might be immediate. When such a need exists, you don't want that money tomorrow, you want it now.

But, let us say that such a person has invested in one of the diamond mutual funds, having sunk all her money into one stone only. And further, let's say that it has only been eighteen months since she's bought. Now she needs to liquidate, to get cash. But, perhaps while other mutual funds have been moving up, this one fund has been on a plateau. Our investor has to liquidate. She would probably sustain a loss.

On the other hand, let's say that instead of buying one diamond in one fund, she bought at least four diamonds, one from each of the funds (which could mean she probably would have bought four lesser-grade diamonds than the one high-grade stone). Now she has four mutual funds to choose from. Perhaps the movement has been in half-carat. She holds her other three stones and sells the half carat for a profit—perhaps a sizeable profit. Now she has the money to sustain herself for a time, a time during which the other mutual funds may move up.

What I'm doing when I say diversity is to suggest the means to reducing the risk of losing money in the short term. I could simply say buy a diamond, any diamond at all, and in five years you'll make a healthy profit. You undoubtedly will. But what about in three years, or even one?

The mutual-fund concept will attain roughly the same long-term goal as buying a single diamond. I suspect that after five or ten years the profit difference will be no more than 4 or 5 percent. But in the short run the difference could be enormous.

Let's say that I have $5000 to invest. I understand about mutual funds and diversification. How should I spend the money?

Five thousand dollars is not a huge amount of money to invest when it comes to diamonds. But it is not too little. (We have many investors who are students who put aside $50 or $100 dollars a month toward diamonds.) Because of the very nature of a book, I cannot say which is the mutual fund to invest in at the time you are reading this material. What is true as I write may be different by the time you read it. I do, however, have this investment tip—one which I think is rather important.

If I had five thousand dollars to invest in diamonds, I would take 70 percent, or $3500, and buy the best diamond I could afford in the largest weight I could afford. I would then take 70 percent of the balance, or $1050, and buy the best diamond I could afford in the next lower grade. I would then take 70 percent of what was left and buy the best diamond I could afford in the next lowest grade, and so on until all my money was invested.

The idea is to give the best possible chance for diversification with the smallest possible amount of investment. Of course, the less money available, the lower the amount of diversification possible. The greater the amount of money available to begin with, the greater the immediate diversification. At the time I write this, I believe that to get really broad diversification would require in the neighborhood of $25,000. Beyond that amount the investor starts to be able to purchase really magnificent diamonds.

Does that mean that if I have less than a minimum of $25,000 I shouldn't invest? Not at all. Remember, the longterm goal is the same. After five years or more the one-diamond investor gets to the same place as the diversified investor. If you have only enough money for one diamond in melee, for example, my suggestion is that you buy it immediately. With the way prices are going, you won't even be able to afford that tomorrow!

CHAPTER ELEVEN

Diamond Profits Today

As I finish this book, the diamond market is in the end of a quiet period. We just had a rapid price appreciation and recently prices have stabilized. In some specific cases they have declined as much as 15 percent. I have been reading articles about the current market in major newspapers and magazines and have been somewhat chagrined by what I've read. Whereas just a few months earlier these same publications were hailing diamond investment, now they appear to be driving the final nail into diamonds' coffin. They speak in terms of the "collapsing" market. The "inability" of DeBeers to maintain prices. The great "sell-off."

I would not feel so bad if I though these newspapers and magazines did not understand what was really happening in diamonds. But we went through the same boom and bust headlines less than a decade ago when the market stabilized in 1974. I would have thought these major publications could learn from past errors. If the investor is to enter the diamond market today with any confidence, he or she should really know what is happening. The purpose of this chapter is to help make things clear.

The Truth About Today's Prices

Beginning in early 1980, the diamond market went through an enormous price appreciation. It was perhaps the greatest single price appreciation in the history of diamonds. The country was in the midst of a financial panic caused by inflation. Inflation had

157

been over 12 percent in 1979 and was over 13 percent in 1980. To the general public, it suddenly appeared that inflation had hit runaway proportions. Twenty-five percent inflation by 1981 was predicted, and 50 percent by 1982.

I have already explained that inflation is the rule—that it is increasing and will continue to do so *in the long run*. But in the short run it has its ups and downs. Back in 1980, however, people were blind to this up-and-down effect. They panicked. There was panic buying in gold and silver, in collectibles and rarities, in land and ... in diamonds. People who had never bought a diamond before in their lives jumped into the diamond market determined to rid themselves of soon-to-be-worthless cash.

The move was correct. But the volume was so extraordinary that no market, including diamonds, could contain it. The sudden unbelieveable demand forced the price of diamonds in all grades through the roof.

That was back in 1980. When 1981 appeared the panic eased. We had a new President and many hoped that he would turn inflation around. The inflation rate itself continued high, but did not turn upward as many had feared. The panic that was rampant only a year earlier faded. Cooler heads and clearer thinking prevailed.

But the market price of diamonds had been run up far beyond where it would have been had the panic not occurred. Some people in their haste to buy had paid too much for their diamonds.

Through our newsletter I warned about the overpriced diamonds late in 1980 and early in 1981. I told our readers that a small part of the one-carat market was over-extended. Those who listened saved their money. But those who bought the wrong stones at the high prices are worrying. Will they get their money out? Is the market going to collapse? Should they have gotten in at all?

They shouldn't worry; the market won't collapse. Although it would have been better not to buy some of the top grade at quite such high prices, it is better to have gotten in high than not at all. Even those who purchased at the top should see profits if they hold their diamonds for the minimum three-year waiting period.

Once the panic abated, diamonds sought their true market prices. Most stones had not been run up overly high and they remained stable in value. Others had been overlooked and they continued to appreciate. The few collector stones priced too high is what has accounted for the scary headlines. In fact, the Salomon Bros. report on diamond values over the past twelve months, released in June 1981, showed stable diamond values over the past year on the average with no declines. Sharp declines were noted for gold and silver.

Anyone who knows anything about diamonds knows that *there is no single market price*. Therefore, it is impossible, and ridiculous, to say the market price has fallen. It's just as ridiculous to say it has risen. The truth is that certain categories of diamonds, certain individual stones, were overbought, and their buyers, unwilling to wait the holding period necessary for profits, sold at less than the prices at the height of the buying panic.

Diamonds *overall* are now rising in price as you read these words! Some are remaining unmoved and, as I indicated, others are appreciating. As is always the case, knowing what to buy shows the profit (or the loss).

Problems with DeBeers

Much has also been said about the alleged difficulties that DeBeers has had controlling the current market. I think these comments demand close scrutiny, not for what they allege, but for what they in reality indicate.

How had DeBeers controlled the market in the past? During times of speculation, the syndicate has released larger quantities of stones to calm the price. But, the demand in 1980 was so great that DeBeers could not release enough material to satisfy it. Neither could the manufacturers cut and polish what was available and get it quickly to the marketplace. So the price rose steeply.

Does this mean that DeBeers lost control? Perhaps momentarily. But did DeBeers lose the ability to support prices? Hardly. If anything, it *temporarily found it difficult keeping them down!* If you have to lose control, that's the way to have it happen.

After the price panic, certain diamonds did in fact decrease in value as I have just explained. This is pointed out by some in the media as further proving DeBeers' lack of control. Not at all. These isolated price drops are a factor of any stable price period. Anytime the price is run up too high, there will be some sellback. It is a reflection of price adjustment.

DeBeers is well aware of what is happening. At recent sights, DeBeers has acted dramatically to reduce the quantity of diamonds released to the marketplace. Fewer diamonds to brokers mean fewer cut and polished. Fewer cut and polished mean higher prices.

It is important to see the forest for the trees in diamond prices. If the investor gets caught up in the emotions of the moment, he or she is lost. The market is like a fine, giant clockwork. It moves slowly, but precisely. And it never stops.

The Israeli "Revolt"

Given the current (as of this writing) policy of DeBeers, it is only natural that many in the diamond manufacturing business are feeling pain. The Israeli brokers in early 1981 threatened to withdraw from the sights unless they received better and greater amounts of merchandise. But, with DeBeers controlling the vast majority of diamond rough, they were forced to accept what was dealt them. Some, however, apparently sought out independent sources of diamonds to make up for the current shortages. Since independent sources even at their peak amount to less than 25 percent of the total market, it is doubtful that this will have much of a long-term effect.

Lack of Quality Material

One item that is truly disturbing and is different from the past stable period is the lack of top-quality material. In the past when the market stabilized DeBeers released fewer diamonds but stones of higher quality. That does not appear to be happening this time.

When asked, DeBeers representatives have flatly stated that they do not have more of the top-quality material. Most of the world's diamonds mines are mature, some in their last years. The world may very well be running out of top-quality material.

Of course, for the individual investor that would be good news. As the best material gets harder to find, those who already own top-quality diamonds will find that their stones are worth more. And newcomers to the investment field will find it expanding as newer grades are opened up to investment. A lack of new top-quality stones will only lead, ultimately, to higher prices.

Given these factors, when is the best time to invest for profit in diamonds?

The wise investor understands the history of diamond price appreciation. A plateau such as we have recently experienced traditionally precedes a price rise. If anything, now is the time to buy, not stay out.

Of course, the wise investor will be selective about his or her purchase. Simply buying indiscriminately will not do. Buying an overpriced diamond still makes no sense. The smart buyer will look for the well-priced diamond in the market, or rely on a reputable investment company to find it.

Diamonds remain the premier form of investment in the world. Nothing else can match their history of performance. Nothing can come close to their desireability. And nothing else can touch their potential. The mistake would be *not* to invest in diamonds.

CHAPTER TWELVE

Diamonds Are Forever

As I write this, many people believe that the world has changed, and changed radically, in the past few years. Budget slashing and hefty tax cuts have suggested that a new era of prosperity is just around the corner. I certainly hope it is but, along with prominent economists, I don't think the basic rules of the game have changed at all.

Tax cuts since the time of the Great Depression have always resulted in increased consumerism. We have generations of Americans who have grown up with the keys to a second car; who learned that to economize means going to the drive-in movie instead of the downtown theater; who believe in spending money, and in *borrowing* to spend. I know very few people who seriously believe that Americans are now going to take their tax cuts and put the money into savings. Rather, they'll do what they've done for decades. They will spend. And spending the tax cuts simply comes down to more dollars chasing limited goods and services. The results, as we have all seen for decades, is increased inflation.

On the other hand, budget cuts mean that the federal government will need to borrow less. Less borrowing puts less demand on the credit markets. It also means that the government won't have to chop down trees quite so fast to make more money!

The result of the tax and budget cuts (along with the tight money policy of the Federal Reserve) is a push-pull situation. Inflation is pushed upward on the one hand, pulled downward on the other. What is the net result for you and me?

As I see it, there are only two possible alternatives. If the planned cuts fail, we'll be back into double-digit inflation. If they succeed, our real rate of inflation (as measured in five-year cycles) won't rise at quite so fast a pace.

There is no other alternative. Those who believe that inflation will end will lose, just as they have been losing for the past fifty years. There is nothing in today's economic package that can bring an end to inflation. Paper assets will continue to depreciate in value, as in the past, and hard assets will continue to appreciate.

Let's consider what that means. We'll take the most popular paper assets—the stock market. If we measure the stock market by the most popular index, the Dow Jones Industrial Averages, we find that it now regularly reaches the 1000 mark, but then it slips backward—often precipitously. It never seems to top 1000 and then soar further upward.

What is curious about this is that it has been the same way for nearly twenty years. During that time inflation has cut our money's value by more than half. If the Dow had kept up, it would today be closing on 3000! Instead, it's still hovering around that same 1000 mark.

The stock market has been inflation negative. Those who invested their money long-term have lost. They were paid back with dollars worth so much less than their original dollars that they often ended with a negative investment.

I don't think this is going to change. We are still going to have inflation and stocks are still going to be inflation negative. The same holds true for other paper investments.

Does that mean you should not buy stocks or other paper investments?

I don't buy them, but then you have to understand my bias: I am totally committed to diamonds. What I am suggesting is that, if in the past you have been totally committed to paper assets such as stocks, you simply reevaluate your position. Perhaps in the future you will want a more balanced portfolio. I'm not saying you should rush out and sell all your stocks. I am saying that you may want to diversify.

The alternative to paper assets is *hard* assets. They are called hard because you can hold the actual investment right in your hand, rather than having a symbolic piece of paper. In this sense they are "legitimate" investments. There are many hard assets besides diamonds, but I want to address the two most popular areas—real estate and precious metals.

Between 1975 and 1980 you couldn't find a person who had a bad word to say about real estate. Never mind that prices of property had barely kept pace with inflation during the 1950s and 1960s. During the late 1970s, real estate got a reputation as a kind of profit king. You just bought property, any piece of property, and you made money.

But what about today? Today's higher interest rates and adjustable-rate mortgages have kicked the supports out of real estate. The thing most of us tended to forget was that, unlike other hard assets, real estate was always highly leveraged. Almost no one paid cash for property. Usually they borrowed heavily to buy—often three-quarters of the purchase price or more. That meant that, in order for real estate to prosper, there had to be a steady stream of easy mortgage money.

Today, as anyone knows who has tried to buy a home, that easy financing has dried up. And with it has gone the rapid price appreciation of property. In some areas the price of real estate is actually declining as sellers are forced to take less in order to offset the difficulty buyers have in financing a purchase.

I don't believe real estate today and in the future will have the shine it did in the late 1970s. It will go back to its earlier long-standing tradition of very slow appreciation. Real estate was yesterday's investment. I'm not suggesting, however, that you go out and sell all your property! There are some advantages, including tax benefits, that real estate still offers. I am saying that today a person whose investment portfolio includes *only* real estate is in almost as bad a position as a person who only owns stocks. The appreciation just isn't going to be there.

The other hard assets that have been popular are gold and silver—the precious metals. Before 1975, Americans couldn't legally invest in gold (they were barred from it by F.D.R. back in 1933), and there was only a small market in silver. Consequently, almost no one considered the investment possibilities.

But then came the great price increases between 1979 and

1980. Gold rose from about $200 an ounce to over $840. Silver jumped from $6 to over $50. Many people jumped on the bandwagon. With precious metals soaring so far so quickly, it seemed the easy road to riches.

But gold and silver are uncontrolled markets. A relatively few speculators had taken over and driven the price up. When these speculators lost control, the markets plunged as quickly as they had risen. Gold dipped to below $400 and silver to way below $10.

What kind of investments are precious metals? For the cunning speculator who can move in and out at precisely the right time, there is obviously money to be made. But for the cautious investor, there is potentially as much money to lose. All today's profit could be wiped out tomorrow. The volatility of the market is simply too great for most people to stand.

If you have been committed to precious metals in the past, I'm not saying you should turn away from them entirely. But common sense dictates that you shouldn't have all your money in such an unreliable place. What if you need to liquidate your investment during a period when precious metals happen to be down in price? If you bought gold when it was $700 and then had to sell when it was $500, you know what I mean.

Now look again at diamonds. In this book I have shown how diamonds function in the marketplace and what the diamond price history has been.

Unlike stocks and other paper assets, diamonds have been inflation positive. If you bought diamonds ten years ago and sold yesterday, you would get back all the money you had invested plus a substantial profit in *real* dollars (dollars that have been adjusted for inflation). If you had bought stocks ten years ago and sold yesterday, chances are the money you got back almost certainly would be inflation negative. After adjusting for inflation it might very well be *less* (in terms of real dollars) than you put in.

Unlike real estate, diamonds have shown steady, strong appreciation over a very long period of time. During the past seventy years, since accurate records have been kept, diamonds have gone up. They went up faster during high inflation periods. During the boom period of the late 1970s, when real estate turned in

165

its best performance in history, diamonds actually outperformed property!

Finally, unlike gold and silver, diamonds have low volatility. Because the DeBeers company exerts such a strong leadership in the diamond market, we find diamond's value does not drop as does gold and silver. When diamond prices reach a new high they may plateau for a period of time, but historically diamonds have not plummeted in value like gold and silver. Should you need to liquidate a diamond investment, you are highly unlikely to find yourself caught at the bottom of a price trough. You should be able to liquidate at a strong price whenever you sell.

Some people believe we may have deflation in the future. Deflation is a condition where the price of everything goes down —the price of your house, your clothes, all personal property, the price of everything! There are virtually no investments with a track record of performing as a hedge against deflation. I personally do not believe there are any investments except diamonds that can serve in both worlds, as a hedge against inflation and a hedge against deflation.

Diamonds do in fact have a track record in both markets. During the Great Depression, diamonds protected individuals. When people were jumping out of buildings, diamond owners weren't. All over America, individuals sold diamonds during the Depression. In many cases, it was the sale of the family gems that made the difference.

It is my opinion that diamonds represent the one answer available today. By owing diamonds, you become a system dropout. You don't play anymore. You march to a different drummer. When you own diamonds, you tie your fortunes to a market that behaves almost exactly as it did in the thirteenth century. In the 1980s, it seems to work better than ever before. And it appears that the diamond market will operate even better in the twenty-first century.

My feeling is that a wise investor will diversify. For certain benefits that it offers, real estate may still be an important part of a portfolio. For the speculator and risk-taker, gold and silver may also be part of that portfolio. And for the conservative blue-chip paper investor, there's always stock.

But a portfolio that does not include diamonds is like a cake without frosting or a car without an engine. Diamonds are the crème de la crème of any investor's portfolio. Diamonds are the shining profit star.

For myself, my commitment is such that I believe a wise investor needs *only* diamonds. As I've indicated, it is possible to diversify entirely within diamonds.

For those of you, however, who are not yet ready to fully commit to diamonds, I challenge you to examine where you are placing your dollars. If a significant portion is not going into a diamond investment (or a diamond God-forbid account), you may be missing the best opportunity out there.

Diamonds are not only *forever*, they are also an investor's best friend.